CRITICAL ESSAYS ON INDIAN ENGLISH WRITING

CRITICAL ESSAYS ON INDIAN ENGLISH WRITING

D. RAMAKRISHNA

ATLANTIC
PUBLISHERS & DISTRIBUTORS (P) LTD

Published by

ATLANTIC

PUBLISHERS & DISTRIBUTORS (P) LTD

7/22, Ansari Road, Darya Ganj,
New Delhi-110002
Phones : +91-11-40775252, 23273880, 23275880, 23280451
Fax : +91-11-23285873
Web : www.atlanticbooks.com
E-mail : orders@atlanticbooks.com

Branch Office
5, Nallathambi Street, Wallajah Road,
Chennai-600002
Phones : +91-44-64611085, 32413319
E-mail : chennai@atlanticbooks.com

Printed in India at Nice Printing Press, A-33/3A, Site-IV, Industrial Area, Sahibabad, Ghaziabad, U.P.

To

Srinivasa

PREFACE

Indian English, like American English or Australian English, has been universally accepted as a unique style of discourse with its own nuances, giving expression to Indian multiculturalism in the works of writers in India or those abroad. Not only the new Indian writers in the West, expatriates, the second and third generation writers, but also the classic authors like A.K. Ramanujan, Nissim Ezekiel, Mulk Raj Anand, R.K. Narayan, and Bhabani Bhattacharya are being interpreted in the old critical mode as well as the current critical styles of multiculturalism, postcoloniality and diaspora. V.S. Naipaul is being interpreted not only as a Caribbean or British author but also as a diasporic writer engaged in a quest for the Indianness inherited by him.

My interest in these critical trends and my personal acquaintance with Mulk Raj Anand and Nissim Ezekiel begun in the late 1970s led to extensive correspondence with them about their work and philosophy of life upto the year 2000. I have made earnest efforts over the years to critically appreciate not only their writings but also those of several other Indian writers in English, while making an in-depth study of Indian multiculturalism in an attempt to place those authors in the appropriate contexts of literary culture.

The following twelve essays, published in research journals or critical anthologies over the years, deal with the general subjects, "Contemporary Indian English Literary Scene," "Multiculturalism and Indian (English) Literature," "Indian

English Prose Writing" as well as the specific authors, A.K. Ramanujan, Nissim Ezekiel, P. Lal, Rabindranath Tagore, V.S. Naipaul, Mulk Raj Anand, Bhabani Bhattacharya, and Shiv K. Kumar. The article on V.S. Naipaul has been written especially for this book.

I am grateful to Dr. K.R. Gupta, Chairman, M/s Atlantic Publishers and Distributors for publishing the book.

I also thank the editors and publishers of the journals and books wherein the articles had been originally published.

D. RAMAKRISHNA

Contents

1

A.K. Ramanujan's Credo*

In spite of A.K. Ramanujan's status as an Indian American, he is an author and scholar whose presence is felt on the literary scene in India and the United States simultaneously. He is different from the expatriates like V.S. Naipaul and Salman Rushdie who are rootless but look at India as exotic. Ramanujan's rootedness in Indian culture and involvement with American culture has resulted in his skilful articulation of both the Indian and the Western ideas with ease. As a poet, linguist, folklorist, translator, and literary theorist, he is one of the world's foremost intellectuals. He is unique in bringing together two great cultures, having been at home in both.

Ramanujan's intellectual position was determined by his multiple interests in Anglo-American New Criticism in the 1950s, French Structuralism, Russian Formalism, and German critical theory in the 1960s and 1970s, and some aspects of French Deconstruction and American and Indian Feminism in the 1980s.[1] That Ramanujan's critical approach is multidimensional is evident from the fact that in his explication of poems, he adopts the formalist literary critical method as well as the contextual concerns of ethnography, history and folklore studies. In his explanations of social codes, he depends on social theory, linguistics, poetics and cross-cultural studies. Ramanujan occupies a unique position in Indian letters in synthesizing his varied concerns as a scholar in Dravidian languages, linguistics, cultures and as a translator of Classical

---

* *Millennium Perspectives on A.K. Ramanujan,* ed. S.N. Pandey (New Delhi: Atlantic Publishers and Distributors, 2001) 1-16.

Tamil and medieval Kannada poetry with his superb poetic instinct in English language.

I

An author's preferences, attitudes, and ideals may be explicit in his essays and interviews or implicit in his creative writings. The controversy regarding "intentional fallacy" notwithstanding, the intentions of a writer often help us in making a proper assessment of the man and writer. In *Theory of Literature,* René Wellek and Austin Warren describe "extrinsic" approach as that which looks at literature in relation to society, ideas, and the other arts as well as "intrinsic" approach that is concerned with image, metaphor, technique, etc. One has to take into consideration a writer's *oeuvre* in order to make a proper estimate of his objectives. An attempt has been made in the present paper to study Ramanujan's credo by means of a scrutiny of both the "extrinsic" and the "intrinsic" aspects of his writings.

While in his creative writings Ramanujan gives expression to his personal neurosis and existential predicaments, he strives to arrive at a definition of Indianness in relation to the Western ethos in his essays. The creative and the critical aspects of his genius are not at variance with each other. In fact, they constitute the essence of his credo. Ramanujan succeeds in telling the world what is truly "Oriental" about India in his authoritative treatment of Indology, correcting the Western notions about the subject.

As Wendy Doniger says in her Introduction to *The Collected Essays of A.K. Ramanujan,* "before Ramanujan, Indian scholars in the U.S. were merely native informants, but Ramanujan blazed a great path through the centre of Indological studies." To quote her:

> At a time when the American Indological establishment regarded native Indian scholars merely as sources of information about languages and texts, like the raw fibres that were taken from India to be processed in British mills, but seldom as scholars who might have their own ideas about how to process those texts, Raman taught them all how to weave a theory, a folk tale, a poem, a book.... (*Collected Essays* 3)

Doniger maintains that the scholarship on ancient India can be comprehended properly only by means of the different paradigms that Ramanujan's work made possible.

Unlike the Postcolonialist scholars, Ramanujan has no political agenda in his articulations of Indian thought. His contempt for politics is well-known. In a passing reference to Edward Said, Ramanujan says that the discourse on the Orient has become controversial: "Indology is an invention and gift of Western scholarship, an ambiguous gift according to some."[2] Like Postcoloniality, "Orientalism" in the Western discourse had been political in orientation. As an Indologist, Ramanujan has proved superior to the champions of both the discourses, having been more deeply involved than others.

Ramanujan maintains that India is multicultural. As he says in his essay, "Where Mirrors Are Windows: Toward an Anthology of Reflections,"

> I would like to suggest the obvious: that cultural traditions in India are indissolubly plural and often conflicting but are organised through at least two principles, (a) context-sensitivity and (b) reflexivity of various sorts, both of which constantly generate new forms out of the old ones. What we call Brahmanism, *bhakti* traditions, Buddhism, Jainism, *tantra*, tribal traditions and folklore, and lastly modernity itself, are the most prominent of these systems. (*Collected Essays* 8)

In addition to his recognition of India's cultural plurality, Ramanujan underlines the "vast variety of Indian literature, oral and written, over the centuries, in hundreds of languages and dialects" (*Collected Essays* 8). He questions the motto of the official Indian literary academy, the Sahitya Akademi, "Indian literature is one but written in many languages," saying "I, for one, would prefer the plural, 'Indian literatures,' and would wonder if something would remain the same if it is written in several languages, knowing as I do that even in the same language, 'a change of style is a change of subject,' as Wallace Stevens would say." (*Collected Essays* 7)

In "Is there an Indian Way of Thinking? An Informal Essay," Ramanujan says "that tradition and modernity, the Eastern and the Western, are like the two lobes of the brain.

They can co-exist." This is his answer to the protagonists of Postcoloniality. Ramanujan's own stance is that in the Indian way of thinking, there is both subjectivity and objectivity. He disagrees with those who talk about "lack of logical rigour" in the Indian mind. As Ramanujan says,

> They may be using a different "logic" altogether. Some thinkers believe that such logic is an earlier stage of "cultural evolution" and that Indians have not developed a notion of "data" of objective facts. Edward Said's *Orientalism* cites many such European stereotypes about the "Third World." (*Collected Essays* 38)

In the words of Edward Said himself,

> ...the imaginative examination of things "Oriental" was based more or less exclusively upon a sovereign Western consciousness out of whose unchallenged centrality an Oriental world emerged.[3]

Even though Said appears to correct the Western notion of the Oriental, meaning the Eastern, except for a mention of Buddhism, he does not deal with Hinduism or Jainism which constitute the major strands of Indian culture and literature. Ramanujan, in dealing with the essence of the complex Indian culture and literature, goes beyond Said, correcting not only the Western notions but also the limited understanding of Orientalism on the part of Said.

At a time when Indian literature meant Sanskrit, and Sanskrit meant Greek and Latin, Ramanujan arrived in Chicago to join Edward C. Dimock and the other "founding fathers" in enlightening the world about the relevance of Tamil, Kannada, Bengali and the other regional languages (*Collected Essays* 3). In his essay entitled "Where Mirrors are Windows," Ramanujan explains further the term "Indian literatures":

> Various bodies of literary, religious, *sastric*, or ideological materials, as they come into being at different periods, become part of the vocabulary of Indian literatures—Hindu, Buddhist and Jaina texts, especially legends, stereotypes, beliefs and the commonly known controversies among them.... (*Collected Essays* 18)

Referring to the pan-Indian network, a repertoire of types and genres that is trans-regional, Ramanujan says that *bhakti*, *tantra* and folklore relate to each other and also have Hindu, Buddhist and Jain forms—creating overlaps, intermediate genres and indeed a scale of forms (*Collected Essays* 27). In another essay entitled "Some thoughts on 'Non-Western' Classics," dealing with the multiple existences of Indian classics like *Ramayana* and *Mahabharata* in oral and written media, in "classical" and "folk" modes, Ramanujan discounts Western classics like *Iliad* and maintains that only the Bible in its hundreds of translations and myriad uses is comparable to the Indian classics. (*Collected Essays* 118)

Ramanujan took pains to highlight the multilingual and multicultural aspects of India. The American anthropologists like Robert Redfield and Milton Singer coined terms like "Great Tradition" (involving the ancient pan-Indian Sanskrit texts) and "Little Tradition" (seen as local, mostly oral, and carried by the illiterate) and stressed the need for "texts of a culture" in preference to "fieldwork." Ramanujan argues that these terms need modification, and asserts,

> Written and hallowed texts are not the only kinds of texts in a culture like India's. Oral traditions of every kind produce texts. "Cultural Performances" of every kind, whether they are plays, rituals, or games, contain texts, written and oral. In a sense, every cultural performance is a text in itself. (*Collected Essays* 16, 18)

The relation of folklore to performance has been dealt with by scholars like Alan Lomax, Roger D. Abrahams, Dan Ben-Amos and Dell Hymes.[4]

Extensively dealing with the multiplicity of Indian literature, Ramanujan argues that not only written texts but also the oral texts are a part of it. Thus, "Cultural Performance," a "text in itself," is linked with folklore in the various languages of India.

According to Ramanujan, the study of Indian folklore has never been a sharply defined field. Overshadowed by Indology, it has a distinguished intellectual history.[5] In his collection of essays on the Indian folklore entitled *Another Harmony*, he says that folk tales in several Indian languages like Hindi, Telugu, Tamil, and Kannada are part of a complex civilization and they are related to the more immediate social and performance contexts. Ramanujan maintains that Indian culture is "a composite of classical, folk, and popular streams."[6] Popular Culture, despite the use of oral transmission, depends heavily on mass media, transmitted impersonally through "showbiz" salesmanship. On account of urbanization of the modern India, folklore has undergone change as evident in TV and other electronic media, thus tradition changing into modernity.[7]

In his Note to *The Interior Landscape: Love Poems from a Classical Tamil Anthology*, Ramanujan says, "Anyone translating a poem into a foreign language is, at the same time, trying to *translate* a foreign reader into a native one."[8] Instead of translating every poem line by line, he renders a poem phrase by phrase, paying special attention to the images and their placement. And he makes explicit typographical approximations to the inner form of the poem. In his "Afterword" to *The Interior Landscape*, the translator says that the *Cankam* poetry is classified by theme into two kinds: poems of *akam* (the "inner part" or the Interior) and poems of *puram* (the "outer part" or the Exterior). *Akam* poems are love poems: *puram* poems are all other kinds of poems, usually about good and evil, action, community, kingdom.[9] Ramanujan's humanistic concerns are evident not only in his creative writings but also in his essays, lectures and translations. The *akam* poetry, synonymous with love poetry in the Tamil tradition, deals with the inner world, the love of man and woman.

In his Introduction to *Hymns for the Drowning: Poems for Vishnu by Nammalvar* Ramanujan explains his method of translation. As he says,

> To translate is to "carry across": "metaphor" has the same root-meaning. Translations are transpositions; and some elements of the original cannot be transposed at all. For instance, one can often convey a sense of the original rhythm but not the language-bound meter; one can mimic levels of diction, even the word play, but not the actual sound of the words.[10]

In his essay "Classics Lost and Found" Ramanujan says: "The word *translate* is only Latin for the Greek word *metaphor*. Both mean 'carry across'" (*Collected Essays* 189). Despite his awareness of what is lost in translation, Ramanujan largely succeeds in carrying poetry across cultural and linguistic barriers. He quotes John Dryden's description of translation in "The Dedication of Aeneis" as "a kind of drawing after life," steering "betwixt the two extremes of paraphrase and literal translation; to keep as near my author as I could, without losing all his graces, the most eminent of which are in the beauty of his words; and those words, I must add, are always figurative."[11]

Ramanujan is a bilingual poet, equally skilful in writing in Kannada and English. Bilingualism and expertise in Linguistics helped him greatly in cultural transmutation. As Bruce King says,

> The highly metaphoric nature of his poetry partly results from an imaginative translation across cultures by striking unexpected associations, a kind of translator's "metaphysical wit" in the creation of multifaceted images. His work as translator and scholar is a strong influence on the mentality that shapes his poetry and his poetics.[12]

Despite its rootedness in Indian cultural traditions, Ramanujan's poetry can be read on its own as English-language poetry with modern themes and forms. Thus, he achieves a rare blending of the ancient and the modern, the Indian and the American idioms. As in T.S. Eliot, in Ramanujan too, there is continuity from tradition to modernity, a continuity between his poetry, translation, and scholarship.

II

Critics generally look at Ramanujan more as a translator than as a major Indian English poet. But Ramanujan is reported to have said toward the end of his life: "All you have to do is to make it clear that my interest in poetry is central to my being and all my work."[13] As a writer, Ramanujan has not received the kind of recognition that he deserves. A close scrutiny of his *oeuvré* will bring out the variety of his reading and complexity of his creative genius. Bruce King says that Ramanujan's reputation, compared to Ezekiel's or Dom Moraes's, is limited:

> Many critics and Indian poets, including Ezekiel, consider him the best Indian poet but he has not had the same

> general recognition and following as Moraes and Ezekiel, except for his translation from classical Tamil and Kannada.[14]

In fact, Ramanujan's intellectual background and involvement with Indian culture are certainly deeper than Ezekiel's and Moraes's. Even though Ramanujan deals with classical Tamil and Kannada writings, he is at home with the larger Indian ethos. Nissim Ezekiel says:

> India is simply my environment. A man can do something for and in his environment by being fully what he is, by not withdrawing from it. I have not withdrawn from India.[15]

The tension in Ezekiel between his Bene-Israel roots and his Indian "environment" is evident in his writings, but he does not make conscious attempts to relive his past. Unlike Ezekiel, for Ramanujan, despite his "environment" in the U.S., with his roots in India, he is equally involved with both the cultures. For him, the American environment is the "exterior" and the Indian environment the "interior." They are the "two lobes" of his brain, as he says in an anecdote about his father (*Collected Essays* 36). As Ramanujan says,

> English and my disciplines (linguistics, anthropology) give me my outer forms—linguistic, metrical, logical and other such ways of shaping experience; and my first thirty years in India, my frequent visits and field trips, my professional preoccupations with Kannada and Tamil, and folklore give me my substance, my "inner" forms, images and symbols. They are continuous with each other, and I no longer can tell what comes from where.[16] (Cited in Parthasarathy 95-96)

Referring to the formative influences of Tamil poets on him, Ramanujan says that in their writings he discovered

> ...the landscapes, the personae, the appropriate moods, all become a language within language. Like a native speaker, he makes "infinite use of finite means," to say with familiar words what has been said before; he can say exactly what he wants to, without even being aware of the ground-rules of his grammar.[17]

Ramanujan is also indebted to Kannada Bhakti poets. As he says,

> The traditional tune-beat, like the ritual gesture, was felt to be learned, passive, inorganic, too well organized to be organic. Here, too, the *stharava*, the standing thing shall fall, but the *jangama* shall prevail.[18]

These shaping influences from Indian culture, coupled with the Western influences, have contributed to the complexity of Ramanujan's poetic genius.

As Bruce King says, "His Indianness is a part of his past, (with which) he is inextricably linked as he changes and develops."[19] It is continuity, not conflict for the poet. In the words of Ramanujan, "Just as our biological past lives in the physical body, our social and cultural past lives in the many cultural bodies that we inherit—our languages, arts, religions, and life-cycle rites" (*Collected Essays* 184). Like his biological past, the poet's cultural past continues to live. It is all the more palpable in Ramanujan due to his frequent visits to India in addition to his continued intellectual preoccupation with Indian culture while in the U.S. S. Nagarajan's statement about Ramanujan's "uprootedness" since he is a "marginalized" man sounds commonplace and naive: "The poet is haunted by a sense of irrecoverable loss and of the transitoriness and insubstantiality of his uprooted life. It is the poetry of the marginal man par excellence."[20] Nagarajan has surely missed the essential Ramanujan. Nagarajan's view about Ramanujan's "alienation" is similar to S.G. Jainapur's: "There is a deep sense of alienation in his poetry.... He felt intensely about his cultural roots when he began to live on alien soil. This seems to have pushed him back to a Hindu ethos in his poetry."[21] These commonplace statements of critics only betray a lack of proper understanding of the complex genius of Ramanujan who has successfully brought together the Indian and the Western sensibilities.

The modernist English influences of Ezra Pound and T.S. Eliot helped Ramanujan to avoid the abstractions of the post-Independence Indian English verse. In *Second Sight* he successfully fuses the forms and tropes derived from poets like William Carlos Williams, Wallace Stevens, and W.B. Yeats with the traditions of ancient Tamil and medieval Kannada poetry. Ramanujan avoids the "monism" of the "pan-Indian Sanskritic Great Tradition" since he believes that "cultural traditions in India are indissolubly plural and often conflicting" (*Collected Essays* 8). As he asserts, "India does not have one past, but many pasts." (*Collected Essays* 187)

As Jahan Ramazani says, referring to Ramanujan,

> Like the postcolonial or migrant subject, torn out of one cultural context and inserted into a new one, the eye that blinks in a new head or the heart that beats in a new chest cannot always adapt with ease to its new surroundings.[22]

It is difficult to put Ramanujan's writing in the straight jacket of postcoloniality. Terms like "displacement," "transfer," "migration," and "alienation" are typical of the postcolonial studies. Ramanujan is certainly an exception as a writer functioning in an alien climate containing both the Eastern and the Western sensibilities within himself. As he says in an interview,

> The past never passes, either the individual past or historical past or cultural past. It is with us...the disconnection is as much an understanding of the past as making the connection. And the living in the present have to see both.[23]

Central to Ramanujan's vision is continuity, past and present, tradition and modernity acting on each other endlessly. Gayatri Chakravorty Spivak says that cultural reversal and displacement results in "the binary opposition, the Western intellectual's longing for all that is not West,...the so-called non-West's turn toward the West."[24] Ramanujan is unique in his ability to contain within himself the binaries, explaining the East to the West and the West to the East with perfect equanimity.

Ramanujan is opposed to the "hypocrisy" of the Indian mind on account of his great concern for the true Indian values. In "Prayers to Lord Murugan," he laments the dichotomy between the inner culture and the outer manifestations: "our blood is brown/our collars white," both in contrast to the Red God:

Lord of the sixth sense
give us back
our five senses...

Deliver us O presence
from proxies
and absences
from Sanskrit and the mythologies

of night and the several
roundtable mornings
of London and return
the future to what
it was.[25]

Ramanujan rejects the abstract and the spiritual in preference to the realities of the Indian life. He wants to highlight the real India free from old myths, abstraction of dead languages and highfalutin talk about political gatherings like the Round Table Conference in London. Ramanujan uses irony to comment on the falsehood of modern Indian mementoes and legends like rajas posing for photographs standing over tigers, and legends like "the peacocks we sent in the Bible/to Solomon."

As an Indian English poet, Ramanujan is unique in integrating the Indian and the Western images. Referring to "Prayers to Lord Murugan," he says that it "could not have been written if I did not know Classical Tamil forms, and even some of the images there."[26] He also stresses the importance of the forms of Classical Tamil poetry and how he tried to adapt those forms in his English poems:

> I prefer the Classical. A typical "Sangam" poem has well-defined, well-wrought complex form. It has an articulate body of convention behind it. The image is not flaunted here but is sharp and pointed.[27]

In his use of the Classical Tamil forms, Ramanujan prefers sharpness of the images. In his English poetry, this use of language is fused with its modern Western counterpart. It is like the use of images by T.S. Eliot and Ezra Pound. In the first section of "Prayers to Lord Murugan," Ramanujan deals with the deep sense of loss in the modern world because Lord Murugan has lost significance in a spiritually bankrupt world. These images of the spiritual bankruptcy of the modern world remind us of the images used by T.S. Eliot in *The Waste Land*. As Edward C. Dimock, Jr., says, in "Prayers to Lord Murugan" Ramanujan attempts "to use human and concrete forms to express the ultimate yet intimate nature of the religious experience."[28] This "religious experience" is not abstract but related to the modern existence.

In one of his interviews, Ramanujan talks about his use of language in poetry and also the plastic quality of poetry:

> Everybody uses language, yet when I use it, I must use it in such a way that it says something new, innocent. Language is full of stock phrases, cliches—you fall back on them whenever you are really thinking. It is exactly like perception.... The words, when they appear in a particular order, surprise you, as though you had never seen them before. That's when you know you can't change it any more.[29]

The sharpness of the image in Ramanujan's poetry is not only like the one in Classical Tamil poetry, but also in the Western writing, as in Ezra Pound's poetry. As Ezra Pound says, "Image is more than an Idea. It is a vortex or cluster of fused ideas and is endowed with energy."[30] If we accept the fact that Ramanujan's poem is replete with images, we shall acknowledge the presence of multiple ideas in it, particularly due to his multicultural vision. In the manifesto of the Imagist Movement, published in 1913, Pound emphasizes: "(1) Direct treatment of the 'thing' whether subjective or objective; (2) To use absolutely no word that did not contribute to the presentation."[31] Also, in a companion article signed by Pound, there is an interesting elaboration: "An 'image' is that which presents an intellectual and emotional complex in an instant of time."[32] According to S. Nagarajan, there is distortion of ideas and limitation of the range of feelings in Ramanujan's use of images since there are different levels of achievement in the same poem.[33] What Nagarajan seems to take as a deficiency in Ramanujan is actually multiplicity of meaning in the poet. Bruce King is more convincing when he says, "His poetry is rich in images and cultural echoes—words reflect and interact with other words—a wide variety of associations from more than one culture and from various historical periods."[34] Thus, what is significant in Ramanujan's images is the cultural resonance, not limitation of the range of feeling. This multiplicity of meaning in Ramanujan's images is the result of his deep involvement with both the Indian and American cultures in addition to his wide-ranging scholarship in cultural anthropology and folklore.

Parthasarathy refers to Ramanujan's "eye for the specific physiognomy of an object or a situation which he then reveals with telling detail."[35] This eye for detail results in the concreteness of the image. In "The Striders" Ramanujan presents the concrete New England water-bug image:

> This bug sits
> on a landslide of lights
> and drowns eye—
> deep
> into its tiny strip
> of sky.

In "Small Scale Reflections on the Great House" the poet's cataloguing of details like "lame wandering cows," "sons-in-law," "letters" (*Collected Poems,* 96-99) or in "Elements of Composition," "memory," "millennia of fossils," etc. (*Collected Poems* 122) is evidently the result of his scholarly involvement with anthropology. For Ramanujan, "memory" is not confined to the family only, or to something that happened in the present or the past. It is anthropological:

> I pass through them
> as they pass through me
> taking and leaving
> affections, seeds, skeletons
> millennia of fossils records
> of insects that do not last
> a day. (*Collected Poems* 122)

This is how Ramanujan is able to bring his scholarship in anthropology to his observation of life around him.

According to Niranjan Mohanty, "Ramanujan's poetry should not be assumed to have originated from the Hindu or Indian milieu, it should rather be seen from the perspective of the symbiosis of the 'outer' and the 'inner' substances."[36] It will be more appropriate to say that while the Hindu or Indian milieu constitutes the "inner" substance of Ramanujan's poetry, the Western milieu shapes the "outer" substance, the two co-existing. In "Extended Family," Ramanujan compares family members and cultures (*Collected Poems* 169-70). The naked, bathing speaker rediscovers himself in relation to others:

Yet like grandfather
I bathe before the village crow

the dry chlorine water
my only Ganges

the naked Chicago bulb
a cousin of the Vedic sun.

Ramanujan brings together the Chicago bulb and the Vedic sun. America is to India what the speaker is to his grandfather. The chlorinated urban water and a sacred river are juxtaposed in an urbanized and Americanized setting. The poem symbolizes Ramanujan's own status as a member of an "extended family," living simultaneously in different cultures and writing about them.

In "A Poem on Particulars" Ramanujan shows how various trees are connected with the lineage of a "single orange." He suggests that one should be reconciled to the world of flux. As a Hindu married to a Syrian Christian and living in America, Ramanujan is aware of the colonial and postcolonial conflicts. His poems reveal his awareness that the past and the present constantly interact, reminding us of Eliot's "Tradition and the Individual Talent." In "History" Ramanujan shows change as a perspective. The speaker as an adult remembers his childhood. The poem takes the reader into the midst of an action. History becomes a reality of the present. "Small-scale Reflections on a Great House" brings history close to the present. The house is a past, a memory, a tradition.

Continuity is a term that is applicable to Ramanujan's works—within a specific genre like poetry or its relation to others like folklore, language, cultural anthropology. Ramanujan exemplifies the extension of the cultural past into the present not only at the specific Indian level but also the universal. Herein lies his uniqueness as a theorist and writer par excellence.

NOTES

1. A.K. Ramanujan, *The Collected Essays of A.K. Ramanuian* (ed.) Vinay Dharwadker. New Delhi: Oxford Univ. Press, 1999, 9. Hereafter referred to as *Collected Essays* in parentheses.
2. Edward Said, *Orientalism*. London: Routledge & Kegan Paul, 1978, 8.
3. Edward Said 8.
4. Dell Hymes, "The Contribution of Folklore to Socio-linguistic Research" in America. Parades and Richard Rauman (eds.) *Toward New Perspectives in Folklore* (Austin: Univ. of Texas Press, 1972) 45.
5. Stuart H. Blackburn and A.K. Ramanujan (eds.), *Another Harmony: New Essays on the Folklore of India*. New Delhi: Oxford Univ. Press, 1986, 1.
6. Stuart H. Blackburn and A.K. Ramanujan 26.
7. Stuart H. Blackburn and A.K. Ramanujan 27.
8. A.K. Ramanujan, *The Interior Landscape*. Bloomington: Indiana Univ. Press, 1967, 11.
9. *The Interior Landscape* 101.
10. A.K. Ramanujan *The Hymns for the Drowning*. New Delhi: Penguin India, 1981, XVI.
11. *Ibid.*, XVI.
12. Bruce King, *Three Indian Poets*. New Delhi: Oxford Univ. Press, 1991, 10.
13. S. Krishnan, "A Poet's Quest." *Indian Review of Books*, (August-Sept. 1993) 11, 28.
14. Bruce King 8.
15. Nissim Ezekiel, "Naipaul's India and Mine" in Adil Jussawalla (ed.) *New Writings in India*. Harmondsworth: Penguin, 1974, 88.
16. R. Parthasarathy (ed.) *Ten Twentieth-Century Indian Poets*. New Delhi: Oxford Univ. Press, 1976, 95-96.
17. A.K. Ramanujan, *The Interior Landscape* 114-15.
18. A.K. Ramanujan, *Speaking of Siva*. London: Penguin, 1973, 38.
19. Bruce King 8.
20. S. Nagarajan, "A.K. Ramanujan" in Tracy Chevalier (ed.) *Contemporary Poets* (Chicago: St. James Press, 1991) 786.
21. S.G. Jainapur, *Poetry, Culture and Language: Indo-Anglian Poets from Karnataka* (Calcutta: Writers Workshop, 1987) 108-09.
22. Ramazani, Jahan, "Metaphor and Postcoloniality: The Poetry of A.K. Ramanujan," *Contemporary Literature* 39, 1 (Spring 1998) 43.
23. Rama Jha, "A Conversation with A.K. Ramanujan," *Humanitics Review*, 3, 1: 1998, 7-8.
24. Gayatri Chakravorty Spivak, *The Postcolonial Critic: Interviews, Strategies, Dialogues* (New York: Routledge, 1990) 8.

25. A.K. Ramanujan, *The Collected Poems of A.K. Ramanujan* (ed.) Vinay Dharwadker, (New Delhi: Oxford Univ. Press, 1995) 117.
26. Rama Jha 7.
27. Nakulan, "A Meeting with A.K. Ramanujan," *Thought*, 21, 48, 1969, 11.
28. Edward C. Dimock, Jr., *The Literatures of India: An Introduction* (Chicago: Univ. of Chicago Press, 1974) 170.
29. Chidanand Dasgupta, "Suddenly a Phrase Begins to Sing," *Span*. 24, 11 (November 1983) 33.
30. Ezra Pound, "Affirmations," *The New Age*, 16: 13 (Jan. 28, 1915) 349.
31. Quoted in Stanley K. Coffman, Jr. *Imagism: A Chapter for the History of Modern Poetry* (Norman: Univ. of Oklahoma Press, 1951) 141.
32. Stanley K. Coffman, Jr.
33. Quoted in A.N. Dwivedi, *The Poetic Art of A.K. Ramanujan* (Delhi: B.R. Publishing Corporation, 1995) 128.
34. Bruce King 8.
35. R. Parthasarathy 95.
36. Niranjan Mohanty, "Things as They Are: The Poetry of A.K. Ramanujan," *Journal of South Asian Literature* 28, Nos. 1 & 2 (Spring & Fall, 1993) 177.

2

Nissim Ezekiel's Credo*

A writer's preferences, attitudes, and ideals may be explicit in his letters, critical essays, and interviews or implicit in his creative writings. The controversy concerning "intentional fallacy" notwithstanding, the intentions of an author often help us in understanding the man and writer better. Nissim Ezekiel, one of the major figures on the contemporary Indian-English literary scene, has offered valuable insights into literature and life in his letters, critical writings, and interviews. Even though much has been said by scholars in India and abroad about his writings, a somewhat detailed study of his credo is still needed for a proper assessment of his work. In his statements about literature, Ezekiel takes what René Wellek and Austin Warren in *Theory of Literature* call the "extrinsic" approach that looks at literature in relation to society, ideas, and the other arts as well as the "intrinsic" approach that is concerned with image, metaphor, technique, etc. He says in his letter of 27 August 1977 to me: "My interests and concerns have to be judged from the whole or a substantial part of my work." Of course, one has to take into consideration a writer's *oeuvre* in order to make a proper estimate of his objectives. Hence an attempt has been made in this paper to study Ezekiel's credo by means of a scrutiny of a "substantial part" of his work, both critical and creative. Both the "extrinsic" and "intrinsic" aspects have been dealt with.

As critic and creator, Ezekiel advocates cultural synthesis. He has sometimes been criticized as being not authentically

---

* *Nissim Ezekiel: Dimensions of a Poetic Genius*, ed. Surya Nath Pandey (Delhi: Doaba House, 1999) 54-69.

Indian on account of his Jewish backgrounds and urban outlook. However, he could see the essential India in the urban climate of Bombay in which he was born and brought up. In an interview to *Indian Express,* he says: "The problems of Indian writers are strange. They have to make a synthesis between the ancient and modern cultures."[1] In his own case a remarkable synthesis happens between the Israeli and the Indian, the Western and the Eastern, and the urban and the rural.[2] This synthesis in Ezekiel's poetic vision is expressed well in *Latter-Day Psalms*:

> The images are beautiful birds
> and colourful fish: they fly,
> they swim in my Jewish consciousness
> God is a presence here
> and his people are real
> I see their sins. I hear
> His anger.

The poet's "Jewish consciousness" is filled with the everyday reality around him. Ezekiel's anxiety to belong to the Indian scene is evident in all his writings. In an interview, he tells John B. Beston that he would like "to belong even more fully to the Indian scene."[3] Referring to V.S. Naipaul, he tells Beston: "Every writer has to write about his original setting rather than the new setting."[4] This conviction can be seen in all of Ezekiel's writings. In his interesting review of Naipaul's *An Area of Darkness,* he says: "A man can do something for and in his environment by being fully what he is, by not withdrawing from it. I have not withdrawn from India."[5] In "Background Casually," the poet says:

> I have made my commitments now.
> This is one: to stay where I am,
> As others choose to give themselves
> In some remote and backward place.
> My backward place is where I am.

Ezekiel stresses the need for a literature of cultural contact on a global scale. While criticising Ruth Prawar Jhabvala's *Heat and Dust* as a misrepresentation of Indian reality, he says that study of the literature of cultural contact is "the cause not merely of intercultural understanding but of humanity and its future."[6] In order to appreciate cross-cultural literature, the reader should have the proper sensibility, capable of understanding the basic human issues. Referring to Berdyaev's views on creativity and culture, Ezekiel says that the poet should be "authentically a creator, and not merely a cultural imitator."[7] While admitting that the poet may choose to play "certain roles," he feels that "these roles are secondary." Thus poetry is essentially universal in its appeal.

Michael Garman is not convincing when he says: "...knowing only English, Ezekiel is to some extent isolated from an Indo-Anglian tradition that has been heavily reliant upon Indian-language poetry."[8] It is doubtful whether all the contemporary Indian poets writing in English have really gained insights into Indian-language poetry. Much depends upon the sensibility of the individual poets. Ezekiel says: "I've always wanted to translate Indian poetry, one of my service functions in life so to speak."[9] He has indeed been doing considerable work in that direction, rendering English translations of poetry in Marathi, his mother tongue.

Ezekiel says that while trying to achieve self-realization through experience of life, man is engaged in a relentless search for identity. In "Something to Pursue," he says: "That I may see myself/No longer unresolved,/But definite as morning." Exhorting Indian youth to be truly Indian, he says: "All growth independent of one's environment has an alienating effect. It's like living in the woods and dreaming all the time of the mountains or the other way around."[10] Ezekiel's preoccupation has always been with an avoidance of both "the sophistication of the rootless" and "the parochialism of the native."[11] Consequently, a writer like him is often more Indian than most others who are unduly ostentatious about their "Indianness."

In an essay entitled "Censorship and the Writer," Ezekiel says that writers should enjoy absolute freedom, acting as "witnesses to the truth within them."[12] In another essay on "The Promotion of Literature," he maintains:

> Literature is wholly concerned with the discovery and expression of truth whereas any machinery for promoting literature attaches importance to prestige, reputation,

> glamour, and extra-literary aspects of writing such as real or alleged piety and national-traditional myth-making.[13]

The "discovery and expression of truth" in literature is an entirely personal experience for the writer. It cannot be done under official patronage. This view concerning the individuality and preeminence of the creative genius is indisputable. The society that promotes literature should aim at "the development of the human sensibility."[14] Even while dealing with the agencies of mass communication like the AIR and *Doordarshan*, Ezekiel maintains that professionalism and creativity "have to be built into the structure of the organization as human values."[15] In "Uncertain Certainties," he refers to "the urge, the call, so to speak, to maintain a link with our experience of ourselves."[16] This is the "truth within" that he emphasizes elsewhere. What Ezekiel means is that the writer should be a man of convictions, unholding human values. He is, in brief, a "man speaking to men," as Wordsworth puts it.

In all of his writings, Ezekiel stresses the centrality of man in the universe. As he says in "Uncertain Certainties," "Spiritual illumination and religious ecstasy are too rare to be even mentioned, and not accessible enough in their discipline and techniques to serve as norms for the sort of human expression I have in mind."[17] Even though, in this essay published in 1975, Ezekiel discounts "spiritual illumination" in creative writing, his later writings make it abundantly clear that religious experience and human expression are not after all incompatible. Referring to Sir Henry Harcourt Reilly in *The Cocktail Party,* he says: "The folly I am referring to lies in the deliberate distortion, the denial of human vitality in the course of spiritual illumination."[18] Thus it is "human vitality" that makes "spiritual illumination" meaningful. In "Morning Prayer," the poet prays, "Whatever the enigma,/The passion of the blood,/Grant me the metaphor/To make it human good." The greatness of poetry lies in its humanizing power.

Ezekiel was atheist and rationalist from 1942 to 1967. In April 1967 he had his first LSD trip—the voyage of discovery of pilgrimage to the centre of life—during his second trip to the United States. In an interview, he told Anees Jung in 1968 that it would be possible to treat LSD as "a starting point for self-transforming processes." The LSD trip is akin to a religious experience: "I believe that it is a transcendental experience or very close to it. The sense of the presence of God during my LSD 'trips' is overwhelming from time to time."[19] Later, in 1977 he told John B. Beston: "Already the seeds of something else are present in my consciousness."[20] Finally it was in 1978 that Ezekiel's masterpiece *Latter-Day Psalms* appeared. Thus the religious strain in his personality found its ultimate expression in his later poetry.

Ezekiel recognizes "the primal stuff of which poetry and mysticism are made."[21] However, he is opposed to the vagueness of the mystical poetry of Sri Aurobindo on account of the "Asiatic vague immensities" of the mystic and the confusion between art and ideology: "Vision becomes a substitute for logic and analysis. The experience of poetry is replaced by ideology, in this case that of evolutionary mysticism."[22] Ezekiel's objection to an ideological presentation of religion in literature is akin to Eliot's position.[23] In his estimate of T.S. Eliot, he recognizes the poet's "central poetic and spiritual concern" as well as the "theme of human destiny."[24] Like Eliot, Ezekiel too is a religious humanist. As Eliot puts it in "Religion and Literature," "For the great majority of people who love poetry, 'religious poetry' is a variety of minor poetry; the religious poet is...leaving out what men consider their major passions, and thereby confessing his ignorance of them."[25] Eliot, while generally agreeing with this view, says, "The author of a work of imagination is trying to affect us wholly, as human beings."[26] As for Eliot and most moderns like him, for Ezekiel too the religious element in literature reveals the writer's moral concerns.

In "Poetry as Knowledge" Ezekiel differentiates between the way poetry is taken by a poet as being purely "subjective" and the way it is taken by others including aestheticians as "data for generalizations."[27] Elsewhere he says that subjectivity is sometimes common to both the creative writer and critic:

> The nature of the subjective, in particular cases, becomes a necessary part of every critical discussion. When it is

> substantial and not superficial, it is an important contribution to the understanding of a creative work. The subjectivity of the critic is then on par with the subjectivity of the creator. Both are equally creative and critical.[28]

While a certain degree of subjectivity in the critic may be essential to comprehend the creative process, excess of it is detrimental to critical evaluation. Referring to Wordsworth's "The Solitary Reaper," Ezekiel says: "We still do not know the experience till such time as we appear to have passed through a process resembling that implied in Wordsworth's poem."[29] Thus the critic should be able to relive imaginatively the experience rendered by the poet. Irving Babbitt considers the true relation between creator and critic. While the creator differs in having "a mysterious and incommunicable gift," he, like the critic, should have the perception of the "human" and the "ethical." Babbitt concludes that "It is in their common allegiance to standards that critic and creator really come together."[30] Thus critic and creator are engaged in a common quest of the human and the ethical. Central to Ezekiel's credo as critic and creator is the same quest.

Ezekiel stresses the significance of the inner life, the journey into the interior. The escape into one's inner life as a means to attain freedom has been a concept common to both ancient and modern life. The conscious awareness of such a means has added a new dimension to modern experience. John Dewey has shown this in his discussion of Santayana:

> Mr Santayana is a thinker whose intent and basis are at one with classical thought. But if we note the importance assumed in his thinking by the "inward landscape," there is before us a measure of the pervasive influence of the kind of experience that was seized upon by Romanticism as the exclusive truth of experience.[31]

Ezekiel's own concern for the journey into the self, the "inward landscape" constitutes his "romanticism" as a modern writer. K.D. Verma says that *The Unfinished Man* is both contemporary in its psychological and social aspects and that "one discerns in it a hidden and powerful yearning of the spirit, somewhat like the Romantic nostalgia, for the lost home which is the world before the fall."[32] While the Romantic note in Ezekiel is unmistakable, Verma is stretching his point too far in suggesting the theme of fall.

In an interview, Ezekiel says that "a poet has to be in love with poetry." Referring to his early poems, he says that they are not merely love poems, and adds: "If I seem to 'advocate' male-female relationship, I am surely in a perennial human tradition that cuts across all national and cultural boundaries."[33] The love in poetry is no taboo; it is the rendition of a "perennial human tradition." Ezekiel also feels that "a dynamic relationship" between "reality" and "mere imaginative constructions and commentaries" is essential since "one cannot invent in the void."[34] His views on love in poetry and the relationship between reality and imagination remind us of Robert Browning's. It is the imaginative harmonization of background that makes Browning's love poetry so exquisitely dramatic. While expressing no great admiration for the Victorian poet, Ezekiel says in a letter of 27 November 1977 to me: "The phrase 'imaginative harmonization of background' appeals to me. I hope it is true of my poetry to some extent." Even though Ezekiel does not consciously employ the dramatic technique like Browning, nevertheless there are traces of the dramatic imagination in some of his poems, He further says in the same letter: "To the extent I have used dramatic techniques, they have been unobtrusive, minor ways of enriching the poem."[35] To John B. Beston's question as to how he would feel about his dramatic work, Ezekiel says: "I feel I have to live twelve lives simultaneously. But my focus has always been on myself as a poet."[36] Referring to "Poster Poems," he says: "I want to live many different lives. The Poster Poems touch various aspects of a personality that can't find a balance and moves in different directions."[37] Ezekiel's statement sounds like an echo of W.B. Yeats's: "It is myself that I remake." As in Yeats, in Ezekiel too, the constant reenacting of the self lends dramatic significance to the poetry.

According to Ezekiel, "Poetry as propaganda is equally suspect" like "versified knowledge."[38] Knowledge in poetry is implicit and inseparable. It is not for its own sake but is integral. And, as he declares, "A poem empty of knowledge is a poem that merely skims the surface of life."[39] In fact, as Austin Warren puts it, "Poetry is a form of knowledge."[40] Even though Ezekiel is opposed to propaganda and ideology in Poetry, he recognizes the importance of ideas. He says, "Ideas are necessary in poetry but a mere formula will not do. The poet has to relate ideas to the material of his individual poems so that they are not dissipated in mere statement but give meaning to those materials."[41] Ezekiel admires W.H. Auden for incorporating the major ideas of the modern world in his poems but finds fault with him for subordinating sensibility to ideas. Ideas should not go counter to "the normal instincts of humanity." While dealing with an idea, the poet cannot afford to ignore images. As Ezekiel says in "Poetry Reading," the echo of the image "swells that message from another shore." The image, presented in the concreteness of a "silver coin," represents an abstract idea. John Crowe Ransom is of the view that "thing *versus* idea does not seem to name an opposition precisely. Then we might phrase it a little differently: image versus idea."[42] Thus image and idea are integral. Through the poem, external reality is translated into internal ideality. The reality embodied in a poem is linked with the reality of the being.

In "Poetry" Ezekiel says: "I would be/In poetry defined/ As in reality I should be so." But this reality is greater than actuality. As the poet puts it in "Hymns in Darkness," "Belief will not save you,/nor unbelief/All you have/is the sense of reality,/unfathomable/as it yields its secrets/slowly/one/by/ one." Thus poetic reality is "unfathomable." Under the influence of Rainer M. Rilke, Ezekiel feels that poetry requires complete silence and solitude to express the profundities of life: "In silence is simplicity,/Expressed through speech, reality" ("Speech and Silence"). Agreeing with Eliot's view that "the poetry does not matter," Ezekiel says that "through poetry we experience a reality that is surely greater than the poetry. But then only great poetry can point to a reality greater than itself."[43] T.E. Hulme has declared that the artist must be able to transcend appearance to perceive a reality behind it.

In a brochure accompanying the third exhibition of *Poster Poems* and *Poster Prayers* at Gallery Chemould in Bombay, Ezekiel says that he does not intend his poems "to compromise with the poster medium by being invariably simple and direct... I chose to take the risks of complexity, compression and stylistic free-wheeling, particularly in the treatment of certain mystical or metaphysical perceptions." The poet presents the traditional religious and metaphysical concepts by means of a synthesis of the verbal and the visual. To Ezekiel, experience is "the primal stuff of which poetry and mysticism are made."[44] Thus poetry need not entirely reject mysticism while presenting life. The poet can make use of the visual arts in the process of such an integration. In the brochure during the exhibition at Gallery Chemould, Ezekiel also says: "My 'technique' was to write each poem first at some length and then to cut it drastically till only an image remains." Visual presentation contributes to the immediacy and intensity of the image. Ezekiel's concern for technical perfection is clear. In his letter of 27 November 1977 to me, the poet says, "Certainly any poet is better understood by insights into his technique. But a first or rudimentary understanding is possible without much awareness of technical devices used by the poet." The poet, like the technician, works meticulously in shaping the poem. Ezekiel asserts that his poetry is not "a mere hodgepodge of devices and lyrical emotions. I work carefully to be appropriate to maintain a tone, to prevent anomalies or incongruities." The poet is basically an artist not in employing art devices as external features but in chiselling out his poem as an artist does, aiming at perfection. As Ezekiel says in his letter of 19 May 1984 to me, "Art is relevant to poetry but obliquely, not in some ideological way." Nevertheless, he is emphatic (in his letter of 27 November 1977 to me) that "In general life is and has to be greater than art, preceding it and retaining its supremacy." Thus in his view, art too, like literature, should be a means of human expression.

Ezekiel has written at length about the creative process and the nature of poetry. However, as he puts it in his letter of 27 August 1977 to me, "I am particularly against extremist and dogmatic theories of how poetry is written." In "Uncertain Certainties," he says that artistic creation flows past the "elusive void within us," or the "true self" which is close to our daily life: "The impulses that arise there are phantoms of our existence, and we try to convert the phantoms into realities so that we may cease to be haunted by them."[45] These phantoms of existence are viewed in terms of the "eternal now." In "Furies" he says: "Neither as enemies/nor as friends/ do my furies/leave me alone." And in "Poetry Reading," the poet's demons wore "angelic wings," showing him "monstrous truths of moral law" governing man's life on earth.

The poet is no mere "trader in paradoxes,/ally of the dialectic" ("Dilemma"). He is a meticulous artist concerned with details like the "word," "image," etc. According to Ezekiel, what is involved in the very process of writing is "a progression from the known to the unknown through the medium of words."[46] In "Poet, Lover, Birdwatcher," he says: "The best poets wait for words." The word, the fundamental element of the poem, conveys meaning by means of suggestion and connotation. It stirs the reader's feelings through the enveloping atmosphere of associations. T.S. Eliot has referred to "words perpetually juxtaposed in new and sudden combinations" in the poem. The poet is distinguished from the common people in the use of words. In fact, Yvor Winters has gone a step further in saying that "Poetry, as nearly as I can understand it, is a statement in words about a human experience."[47]

In "Poetry as Knowledge," Ezekiel says: "Poetry that is not experienced as poetry but as thought is disappointing and frustrating."[48] He recognizes the elusive nature of poetry: "...it is impossible to have a full and final view of the nature of poetry."[49] Poetry is something greater than a mere poem: "A poem is an episode, completed/In an hour or two, but poetry/ Is something more" ("Poem"). Poetry is elusive because it is the embodiment of truth in its personal and universal aspects. Ezekiel disagrees with I.A. Richards who says that the statements of poetry are pseudo-statements. According to Ezekiel, poetic truth is not pseudo-truth and it "may be located anywhere between the strictly personal and the universal."[50] In fact, the question of the poetic truth has engaged the attention of critics from Plato and Aristotle to the moderns. The poet, in Shelley's view, is in touch with the eternal pattern of things that underlie all reality.

Ezekiel feels that major poetry can dispense with conceptual thinking. The conceptual character of thinking is concealed by the form, which is "not a dress, manner or style but an organic, integrated growth, a basic mode of expression in which thinking is not separate from all the other elements that go into its making."[51] This brings us to the question of form and content relationship. In "A Note on Form in Poetry," Ezekiel says that he would like "to let the form develop as the poem develops. The problem is how to make a poem well without ending up as a merely well-made poem. A form is also, among many things, a happening. It must seem inevitable."[52] Thus the relationship between form and content is organic. Form is not an external framework into which the content could be fitted. Ezekiel adds: "In writing a poem, I want to make or construct a pattern of meanings."[53] The evolution of a pattern of meanings is the form of the poem. In T.E. Hulme's view the organic form of a poem is a function of intuition. The artist must be able to transcend appearance to perceive a reality beyond it. The organic nature of form has been stressed by Coleridge too, who declared that nothing that is "superadded" for ornament or decoration, can really please in a poem.

Ezekiel agrees with Eliot that Tennyson and Browning ruminated in verse, while Donne thought with his body.[54] Eliot objects to the ornate in Tennyson and the bizarre in Browning. Ezekiel too is averse to obscurity in modern poetry. As he puts it:

> Attacks on obscurity in poetry are generally dismissed as anti-intellectualist. But there still remains a case against always giving obscurity and difficulty the benefit of the doubt on the ground that some profound truths can be expressed in no other way. Too many poets in the twentieth century offer only the difficulty and not the profundity, though it is not considered respectable in literary circles to say so.[55]

Modern writers have a tendency to justify the complexity of their writing on the ground that modern life is complex. However, the complexity can be presented in deceptively simple form, as sometimes the profoundest philosophical truths are presented. In his Preface to *Lyrical Ballads,* Wordsworth says, referring to the language of poetry, that "our elementary feelings co-exist in a state of greater simplicity" and consequently may be "more accurately contemplated, and more forcibly communicated." Ezekiel advocates simplicity of thought and language in modern poetry. Of course, the nineteenth-century poet was concerned with the language of the rustics. In "A Note on Form in Poetry," Ezekiel extends the concept of simplicity to form in poetry. In rhythm, he would aim at "the natural, the flowing, the direct and the informal or conversational." He is aware that "if taken to extreme or practised as a doctrine, this can lead to prolixity or journalese." In his letter of 27 November 1977 to me, the poet says: "...even the most complex of my poems are relatively simple and direct, judged by the norms of difficult poetry properly so-called." In "Art Lecture," he evokes simplicity in his desire to find the exact name: "The devious word dissolved, the mirror true." In "Credo," one of the "Postcard Poems," he hopes "to describe anguish/in a soft voice,/in the simplest statements/to body forth the passions." In Wordsworth's view, our passions, our elementary feelings, "co-exist in a state of greater simplicity." Ezekiel's aversion to obscurity is evident in his Poster Poems. Each prayer, emanating from the recesses of his inmost being, finds expression in simple diction: *e.g.*, "follies...fresh as flowers," and the desire of the self to "fly with the sparrow." While the Romantic poet realizes the Primordial in Nature, a modern poet like Ezekiel seeks it in the urban climate—the "kindred clamour close at hand" ("Urban"). In "Perspective," the poet goes beyond "the safer paths of men" and "rides into a marsh to see the Grail."

Ezekiel is opposed to incoherence and confused thinking in literature and art. Since "normal modes of communication do not work when certain kinds of insight (inspiration)" are experienced, obliqueness may be resorted to by the writer. However, obliqueness does not mean obscurity. An idea gains significance when it is presented obliquely: "But even the simplest idea has dimensions which verbal clarity distorts or altogether destroys. Many a clarified idea is an empty shell."[56] T.S. Eliot has commented upon "that perpetual slight alteration of language, words perpetually juxtaposed in new and sudden combinations," which occur in poetry. This is the way the poet uses the metaphor as a device for expanding meaning, for producing ambivalence. Ezekiel has said that "The body of poetry is emotion,"[57] and that the poetic illusion can be presented by means of metaphor. As I.A. Richards has pointed out, all of the subtler states of emotion necessarily demand metaphor for their expression.

In his essay entitled "Should Poetry be Read to Audiences?" Ezekiel says that the poet "reveals in his reading, unconsciously, his attitude to the poetry and to his audience. I suppose the best attitude is one of detachment, aimed at total communication but maintaining a certain purity and simplicity."[58] Yvor Winters in "The Audible Reading of Poetry" insists on "dramatic declaration" and says: "A poem calls for a formal reading, partly because the poem itself is of its own nature a formal statement, and partly because only such a reading will render the rhythm with precision."[59] The poet's chief concern is a proper communication of sound and sense. Quoting Eliot's words with reference to Dante that "genuine poetry can communicate before it is understood," Ezekiel says that "what is so communicated is less than what is understood, that understanding alone completes the communication in so far as it can be completed."[60] In fact, what is involved in the process is "a progression from the known to the unknown, through the medium of words."[61] The poet communicates to the reader not only messages concerning actuality but also ideality. I.A. Richards has told us how words can communicate attitudes which result in a valuable psychological state in the reader. By causing a proper state of mind in the reader, the poet achieves effective communication of his meaning.

Ezekiel's quest as writer and critic over the years has been for a proper communication of the meaning of life. He has carved a niche for himself in the world of literary art as a practising poet of international standard. His credo is based on sound convictions in respect of both the extrinsic and intrinsic aspects of literature. With an unmistakable sense of Indianness, he has shown that the critic and creator are basically men of refinement presenting the myriad nature of the human spirit.

NOTES

1. *Indian Express,* 7 November 1982.
2. Ezekiel belongs to the Jewish tribe of the Bene-Israel which, as he tells us, must have migrated to India not later than 379 A.D. He has thus imbibed the wisdom of both Israeli and Indian cultures.
3. John B. Beston, "An Interview with Nissim Ezekiel," *World Literature Written in English,* April 1977.
4. *Ibid.*
5. "Naipaul's India and Mine," reprinted in *Journal of South Asian Literature,* Vol. XI, No. 3-4 (Spring, Summer 1976) 203.
6. "*Cross-Cultural Encounter in Literature,*" *The Indian P.E.N.,* Vol. 43, No. 11-12 (Nov-Dec 1977) 6.
7. "Poetry as Knowledge," *Quest,* 76 (May-June 1972) 44.
8. Michael Garman,"Nissim Ezekiel—Pilgrimage and Myth," *Journal of South Asian Literature,* Vol. XI, No. 3-4 (Spring, Summer, 1976): 221n.
9. John B. Beston, "An Interview with Nissim Ezekiel", *World Literature Written in English,* April 1977.
10. *Free Press Bulletin,* 7 October 1974.
11. "Two Poets: A.K. Ramanujan and Keki N. Daruwalla," *The Illustrated Weekly of India,* 18 June, 1972: 43.
12. "Censorship and the Writer," *Seminar* (July, 1963) 7.
13. "The Promotion of Literature," *Indian Writers Meet* (Bombay: The P.E.N. All-India Centre, 1966) 12.
14. *Ibid.*
15. "AIR and Doordarshan," *New Quest,* No. 8 (March-April, 1978) 133.
16. "Uncertain Certainties," *Fulcrum* (November-December 1975) 19.
17. *Ibid.*
18. "Poetry as Knowledge," *Quest,* Vol. 76 (May-June 1972) 43.
19. "LSD: The Meaning of Reality," An Interview with Anees Jung, *Times of India,* 1 December 1968.

    In "Poetry as Knowledge," Ezekiel says: "Drug-induced states of mind in which consciousness is temporarily expanded and intensified have so far not produced any notable poetry."

    In his letter of 7 November 1984 to me, he says that the LSD experience "seemed religious though I had some reservations about it later in terms of practice, actual religious practice as against religious consciousness."
20. John B. Beston.
21. "Poetry as Knowledge" 43.
22. "Sri Aurobindo on Poetry," *The Times of India,* Sunday, 23 July 1972: 9.

Ezekiel says: "Poets who have mystical experiences and project them in verse have occasionally been successful but mystics who write poetry do it badly.... Great religious poetry undoubtedly exists but the greatness is unequally divided between the poetry and religion, while perfect integration between the two is rare. To be good, poetry has to be an independent art." "Poetry as Knowledge" 43.

23. Ezekiel has stated that he admires "the saintly" T.S. Eliot greatly as poet and critic. See "Censorship and the Writer," *Seminar*, July 1963.
24. "T.S. Eliot—A Personal Review," *Quest*, No. 45 (April-June 1965) 18-19.
25. T.S. Eliot, "Religion and Literature," *Five Approaches of Literary Criticism*, ed. Wilbur S. Scott (New York: Collier Books, 1962) 45.
26. *Ibid.*, 48.
27. "Poetry as Knowledge" 43.
28. "Merely Subjective," *The Sunday Observer*, 18 December 1983.
29. "Poetry as Knowledge" 44.
30. Irving Babbitt, "Genius and Taste," *Five Approaches of Literary Criticism*, ed. Wilbur S. Scott (New York Collier Books, 1962) 37-38.
31. John Dewey, Experience and Nature (New York: W.W. Norton and Co., 1925) 229-30.
32. K.D. Verma, "Myth and Imagery in *The Unfinished Man*: A Critical Reading, "*Journal of South Asian Literature* 230.
33. "In Love with Poetry," *Youth Times*, Vol. VIII, No. 17, February 1-14, 1980: 17.
34. *Ibid.*
35. Even though Ezekiel's dramatic writings are limited in number compared to his poetry, his skill as a dramatist is indisputable. As drama critic, he stresses the need for human vitality. The dramatist "should be familiar with the speech habits of the prototypes of the characters in real life" in addition to having "inner knowledge of the stage and its conditions."

    Quoted in Fritz Blackwell, "Four Plays of Nissim Ezekiel," *Journal of South Asian Literature* 272.
36. John B. Beston.
37. *Ibid.*
38. "Poetry as Knowledge" 43.
39. *Ibid.*, 48.
40. Rene Wellek and Austin Warren, *Theory of Literature* (1942; rpt. Harmondsworth: Penguin Books, 1973) 32.
41. "Ideas and Modern Poetry," *Indian Writers in Conference*, 1964: 54.
42. Quoted in Max I. Baym, *A History of Literary Aesthetics in America* (New York: Frederick Ungar Publishing Co., 1973) 296-97.
43. "T.S. Eliot—A Personal Review" 22.

44. "Poetry as Knowledge" 43.
45. "Uncertain Certainties" 19.
46. "Censorship and the Writer."
47. Yvor Winters, "The Audible Reading of Poetry," *Perspectives in Contemporary Criticism*, ed. Sheldon N. Grebstein (New York: Harper and Row, 1968) 134.
48. "Poetry as Knowledge" 46.
49. *Ibid.*, 48.
50. *Ibid.*, 46.
51. "Poetry as Knowledge" 46.
52. Written in response to a request in March 1978.
53. *Ibid.*
54. See "Poetry and Philosophy," *Quest*, No. 50 (1966) 25-30.
55. "Should poetry be Read to Audiences?" *The Sunday Statesman Magazine*, 27 August 1972: 11.
56. "Uncertain Certainties" 19.
57. "Poetry as Knowledge" 47.
58. "Should Poetry be Read to Audiences?" 11.
59. Yvor Winters, "The Audible Reading of Poetry" 136.
60. "T.S. Eliot—A Personal Review" 18.
61. "Censorship and the Writer."

3

Soul-Stuff and Vital Language : The Poetry of P. Lal*

I

In his introduction to the anthology *Modern Indo-Anglian Poetry* (1959), P. Lal finds fault with the vagueness of the "slushy verse" written by poets like Sri Aurobindo:

> ...... This kind of slushy verse is the most dangerous thing that infects our poetry today. It has spoilt a good deal of the Indo-Anglian past; it can without exaggeration spell ruin for the future. For an off-shoot of English poetry trying to establish roots in rocky ground, having a small and gradually dwindling public, such nebulosity in form and substance can be positively pernicious. Even the best Indo-Anglian poets writing now...are not always entirely free from the clutches of soul-stuff.
>
> The temptation to slip into greasy, weak-spined and purple-adjectived "spiritual" poetry always exists; it exists especially in the case of a poet who has failed to realise that the art of poetry is an art as exacting and painstaking as the carving of an original design in ivory, that a poem is not a spasmodic burst of a spasmodic emotion, but a delicate choreographic pattern within a state of balanced tension....

Lal's main contention is that poetry should deal with real life situations, but not with philosophical abstractions. As an art form, it is a painstaking exercise like "the carving of an original design in ivory." Such careful manipulation of poetic

---

* *Indian Poetry in English*, ed. Hari Mohan Prasad (Aurangabad: Parimal Prakashan, 1983) 136-48.

language should contribute to evoking concrete images. The language of poetry should be "vital," whether it is in modern idiom or "ancient," coming close to the "current pattern of speech." In saying that poetry is not "a spasmodic burst of a spasmodic emotion," Lal discounts the romantic conception. Thus he says in his eight-point declaration of poetic independence: "We claim that the phase of Indo-Anglian romanticism ended with Sarojini Naidu." Poetry, Lal adds, should be "free from propaganda" and express the "private voice" in lyric form. However, he admits that "Even the best Indo-Anglian poets writing now...are not always entirely free from the clutches of soul-stuff."

In the second number (1960) of *Writers' Workshop* "miscellany of creative writing," Lal feels that there could be Indian motifs, responses, attitude and trends—the images of rain, peacock and lotus, for example, and attitude like renunciation, resignation and non-attachment. In December 1961, referring to Sri Aurobindo, Toru Dutt, Sarojini Naidu, Manmohan Ghose and Harindranath Chattopadhyaya he conceded that "They provide sufficient provocation to experiment afresh, set new standards, preserve what is vital in the tradition and give a definition to the needs of the present." Thus Lal has embarked on a mission to modernize Indo-English poetry, whatever the seriousness with which he is taken by the ultramodern members of his tribe.

The main objective of the poetry of Sri Aurobindo, against whom Lal's attack is directed, is to attempt a synthesis of the material and the spiritual. Savitri is intended as a symbol of the traditional Indian womanhood, the devoted wife's power to conquer evil in the way of existence. Perhaps the changing concepts of family and womanhood in a Westernized setting make it difficult for the modern Indian to appreciate the significance of Sri Aurobindo's idea. Lal emphasizes "concreteness" under the influence of the Western theory of concrete imagery. However, what sounds abstract to the Western sensibility may sometimes evoke a definite meaning for the Indian. In spite of the kind of "authenticity" of modern experience (be it sexual symbolism or concrete images from everyday reality) that Lal aims at in his own poetry, his essential Indianness lies in the synthesis of tradition and modernity.

Even though he is not concerned with the "soul-stuff" as poets like Sri Aurobindo do, in his own work he presents the essence of the soul in an ethical context. It may be profitable to observe, by means of a broad survey of Lal's poetry, to what extent he is "free from the clutches of soul-stuff."

II

In the poem "T.S. Eliot" Lal pays a tribute to the great master:

....who taught us the use of words,

The voice descanting in the ear.

The influence of Eliot, the "noble father of the new style," on Lal is particularly noticeable in "the use of words," the colloquial speech rhythms with the "syllables of sensuous intelligence." Lal's reflections on the modern city are reminiscent of Eliot:

This night, this summer, in my broken city,
The ghosts of yesterday
populate the blurring panorama of to-day.
See, in the stiffening light,
a crooked leg, thin muscles move in lost delight:
Every night,
pock-marked and inelate,
The haggard Bawd takes a refugee for mate.
("The Refugees at Sealdah Station")

From the stark reality of an urban situation we are led into the mythical realm in "The Bitterest Reason":

There was the bitterest reason Sita wept
The bitterest reason Penelope cried
Penelope had webs to weave at dead of night
Sita had fire to see her through—

The traditional Indian concept of Sita is juxtaposed with that of Penelope, thus presenting a human situation from the perspective of two cultures. Lal's achievement as a poet, like Eliot's, lies not in philosophical abstraction but in the particularity of living experience evoked by the images:

You shall come here as bird or leaf.
Here are afternoon pleasures:
Tea before sunset, and conversation.
("The Rose World")

A bald statement like "This is a rose world" acquires a new dimension of meaning in the line that follows: "Here meaning is in fragrances." Perhaps Lal is as modern as any other Indo-English poet in the evocation of a subtle sensuous meaning through a striking metaphor:

Love, twin-fuselaged,
Sweeps serenely thus
(Weather Report: Unfair)
To passion's terminus
Hand to breast in summer
Savour the moth's bouquet;
Destination: Belonging,
Ticket: One-way.
("A Star to Calling Star")

The economy of language and metaphysical wit (probably under John Donne's influence) make the image vividly realized.

While it is not proper to look for "social consciousness" in Lal's poetry, any judicious estimate of his vision should take into account his concern for the human predicament. In "Darling Talk of Crime" the poet directs his ironic vision toward the deteriorating state of society that makes even love an expensive commodity:

Even my dates with you
Have me upon the hip:
Air-conditioned restaurants
Make exorbitant demands,
The shady waiter too
Compels a bigger tip.

Only love is simple,
Only you are free,
Nothing more expensive than
Youth's liberal clan,
The price of every dimple
A foolish word from me.

Despite the tone of light-heartedness, the poet presents here an authentic experience of modern lovers in a language free from ornamentation. In "Famine" he expresses agony at the indifference of the rich while famine plays havoc with life around:

Ghosts whisper on the staircase at Firpo's,
At Chung Wah they speak over fried rice
    and sweet-and-sour pork;
Sitting near a window with noodles in cream,
The noodles are eyes, gaunt, of an innocent child.
And swing bands on Sunday afternoons
Squeeze light jive for jaded executives in rayon shirts;
He sits by a window and sees, ah, skeletons,
Perform on the floor in a danse macabre.
And the music dissolves, the dancers
Stand in knots and clap, each with a tubercular rattle;
He reads the menu and the bright names murmur;
Saurashtra, Bihar, Cochin, the Sunderbans.

In *Calcutta* Lal exposes the "unreal" nature of contemporary urban life:

Shacks
Upon
Shacks
Ghosts
Merging
Ghosts
Fading
Shuffling
Vanishing
Nothing

Spirits of my fathers
elders of Kapurthala
    remember my exile
    in the city of Calcutta....

Sometimes blending of the unfamiliar with the familiar heightens the "unreal" nature of urban life.

Come, darling, let us set up home
    And ride by regal rikshawwalla
To caverns with an icy dome
    And milk by the goala
And while I chase the good rupee
    At Dharamtalla, darling mine,
You cultivate Society
    And hanging blouses on the line.

These urban scenes expose much that is hollow in contemporary Indian life. On the whole, Lal attempts to create in his poetry a wasteland situation, reminiscent of T.S. Eliot.

III

Even though Lal declared in his manifesto that romanticism in Indo-English poetry came to an end with Sarojini Naidu, his own poetic world is filled with birds, flowers, and fruits in an atmosphere of overwhelming beauty. His stanzas are often illumined by sparkling phrases: "the green continent of earth," "And in the south wind's music/The assonance of grief....," "In a world of footfalls/Her silence is a lily." The world of birds merges with the human in an experience of love:

My love is no less bright
Than these bright birds today
In the diffuse delight
Of sun and wind at play—
("The Privilege")

Sometimes Lal's enthusiasm for the sound of words leaves the reader cold:

My love perhaps and your love perhaps was far
from sensible, even put on a false tan;
the falseness is false no longer:
we have jilted too often, but the doom on
doomsday is certain
("Lying Along this Broken Beach")

However, he is generally capable of manipulating language and image in an impressive manner.

Look, on a golden rose the hunched bee
exhibiting a pose as a cocoon,
silent upon the incessant afternoon
distils its summer share of ecstasy
(the indeterminate turn of either knee
suiting the night jaunt of a tipsy moon);
and, all despair and drunk, drops half a swoon
and with the summer drouses peacefully.
("The Simplest Love")

Like the bird, the rose is a recurring image:

This is a rose world,
Here meaning is in fragrances
And life is the careful delivery of leaf.
This is my friend's rose garden;
No welcomes and no farewells—
You shall be remembered in terms of love.
Stranger, if I should decide
You as attitude, a pose in the delicate air,
I should wonder why roses are fragrant.
But this is my friend's rose garden.
You shall come here as bird or leaf.
Here are afternoon pleasures:
Tea before sunset, and conversation,
Squirrels and homing sparrows.
The meaning of this rose world communicates
Syllables more splendid than life.
("The Rose World")

The Keatsian evocation of the senses is significant. The rose world communicates the ideal of love in "syllables more splendid than life." The world of man merges with that of the roses and birds, resulting in the bliss of love, the experience of the being: "You shall come here as bird or leaf." The mystic state can be attained by dissolving the individual self into something "more splendid than life." Elsewhere in Lal's poetry the bee's progress toward the rose signifies the poet's "encounter with God in a rose garden." The poet's involvement with the beauties of Nature makes him ecstatic about "My green soul...," "Benign sun to my soul...," "Soul is to cage/As love to foe...."

Lal's romanticism is palpable even in his description of a real life situation in "The Refugees at Sealdah Station":

And hearts shall catch, as windows, the concentrated sun,
Dumb heart, speak out and say:
Love being stronger, my passion says:
So many beauties spun
Even from such a lust, as cloud from the ebbing day;

Sometimes the matter-of-fact event acquires supernatural significance:

He dreampt he saw a slow marriage procession
Sneaking into Lake View Road, where
Drumming ghosts melted with Teachers' Agitation.
Nothing remained but a fistful of air.
("Change They Said")

The romantic soul in Lal's poetry is "fixed and immaculate." It is feeling elevated to the level of prayer that constitutes the essence of his writing in this genre:

The child's moon is my truth: in spite
    Of clouds, fear, lust, anger, hate,
    Soul remains fixed, immaculate.
("The Moving Moon at Mussourie")

Sometimes the concreteness of imagery descends from romantic sensualism into sexualism typical of the contemporary Indo-English poet:

Bubbles of bead necklace like a river
Flow through the valley of her opulent breasts
Briefly trapping the touring eye: to the carver
    These sandstone breasts with broken
    Nipples were like apples taken
In token quenching of monumental thirst.
Eyes travel on twin folds on her asking
Belly, in the navel's whirlpool is pulled
Youth of voluptuous innocence, asking
    The same question—why,
    Why is the flesh, why
Belly and navel, innocence and whirlpool, pulled.
Only in lonely dreams is the answer: Fairy,
Yakshi, beloved, stone, girl with feather fan,
Carved in dreams for fits of phallic fury,
    Purge flesh of desire!
    Purge it in pools of fire!
Till, purged, man discover he is immortal stone.
But all in delight! All in sensuous
Delight, Yakshi, with left arm missing, the right
With feather fan, broad thighs feasting the senses,
    Hair in two frozen buns,
    Breasts between whose two suns

A rivery necklace awaits descent of night.
("Yakshi from Didarganj")

The multitude of images employed has a certain restraint, contributing to poetic intensity. However, in Lal's poetry sometimes the collocation of images tends to be monotonous since they do not flow into one another:

Pick up your beauty, beloved, sell
　　any remainder, see if you come out even;
Beauty/I'm told is red, but
　　redder the red of doomsday in heaven.
Delightful philosopher,
　　how many platitudes are constituent to age?
Count them, and throw them, see
　　if the platitudes of doom on doomsday give you
　　courage.
("Lying Along This Broken Beach")

The images alternate between concrete presentation and vagueness, the result being not poetic intensity but inanity.

IV

While P. Lal attempts to present physical reality in a way that appeals to modern sensibility, his basic religious sense is conspicuous. Perhaps this lends depth of meaning to his writing. In "The Letters of Crystal Lips" he presents a human predicament in poignant terms. An extreme tension caused by death of the dear is rendered in a tone elevated to the level of meditation:

My lips grow dry with my husband's absence
In my hair I put a white poppy
For my husband's absence.

There is scent in the air, father
White the waters: the trailing willows are
　　　　　　　　　　　　wand-like reflected;
How sweet the fluting of small-eyed sparrows!
I nourish a white poppy
And take care of my lips.
("The Three Letters of Crystal Lips")

"The Prayer" is a superb instance of Lal's management of the poetic effect by means of symbolism:

Giving what I can give
Of prayer, is a sea shell.
In it the winds live.
Rolling out of reach
The shell discovers the beach,
Just as well.
Hollow the shell, until
Upon the blinding sand
Ocean rumours fill
And fold into a prayer
A breath of lifeless air.
This I understand.
And the shell becomes bird.
It's just as well
Meaning becomes absurd.
Wings, each on each,
Usurp the world of speech.
This is possible.

The rhyming of the lines synchronises with the resonance of the shell filled with the sound of ocean waves. Consequently there is an admirable synthesis of sound and sense. The poet exploits the rich possibilities of the popular belief in the shell, the conch, as a means of elevating the soul in an attitude of prayer. In "Boeing 707 Flight No. 201" the landing of the plane has symbolic meaning. The poem begins with an incantatory note:

Suspended in mid-air
With folded palms, his prayer
Minutes before landing, where
Dark liquid eyes await
He Ram! He Krishna!
He Ram! He Krishna!

And it ends on a note of requiem:

Well, it was a bit like this—
We touched, bumped, seemed to miss
The runway—then a hiss,
A roar, a ball of flame.
Hare Ram! Hare Krishna!

The poet's tone here is different from the ironic stance sometimes he takes while dealing with religious experience.

The spiritual strain in Lal's thought deepens in the poems written in late 1970s. *Calcutta* (1977) is a mature statement on the essence of the spirit unlike the earlier poems in which the emphasis is more on the material, the secular in contemporary Indian life. The image of Mother Theresa determines the atmosphere of the poem. The poet implores her:

> Pray for these ghosts, Mother,
> in the valley of our sorrows
> in the city of my domicile.
> Bless the ghosts who sit in offices
> Bless the broken ghosts
> hunched on benches in Outram Park.
> Bless the ghosts broken
> and unbandaged
> Bless the ghosts broken by guilt
> And ghosts in frayed faded dhotis
> Genuflecting near Kali Mandir
> Bowed and decrepit
> Discarded scraps in the lottery of life.
> ("Calcutta: A Long Poem")

The depth of feeling for humanity and recognition of the need for spiritual solace in the turbulent contemporary life are unmistakable here. The poet wants Mother Teresa to uplift the troubled souls around him. This, in fact, is the kind of "authenticity" of soul's experience that Sri Aurobindo and Swami Vivekananda advocated a century ago.

In his introduction to *The Man of Dharma & The Rasa of Silence* (1974) Lal says:

> In a world ruled by the inexorable laws of cosmic and personal karma, everything comes with its built-in opposite; the best art can do is to provide man with a fleeting glimpse of life's ambivalence and paradox or, if one prefers a more nebulous word, "mystery." A fleeting glimpse which can be a harrowing vision. The true face of this vision is the "rasa of silence." This is the face that Yudhishthira thinks he sees on Mount Meru; that is why he, and not

any of the others, is worthy of being anointed the "man of dharma." In other words, all esthetic relish, and all life-relish too, is rooted in the ultimate experience of silence. (The epigraph) from Rabindranath, Poem 13 of *Shesh-Lekha*, written six days before he died, poignantly underlines the mystery of this ultimate experience.) The mature reader knows that all words, no matter how subtle, are merely an embroidery on the fabric of silence.

This idea of life and art as the "ultimate experience of silence" is central to Lal's poetic and aesthetic vision. His "modernity" is unique in Indo-English poetry on account of this basic aesthetic perception, the "soul-stuff" of his own creative writing. Ironically, while rejecting the older poets, he strives to achieve a synthesis of tradition and modernity for which the older masters also stood in their own times. The "authenticity" of experience which he stresses so much has cultural implications beyond the conscious level. By applying Western standards alone it may not be possible to determine what is "authentic" in the experience rendered in Indo-English poetry. A clash of sensibilities is ever present. On the whole, P. Lal's position as a theorist and practitioner of the art of poetry tends to be paradoxical.

4

Contemporary Indian English Literary Scene*

Contemporary Indian English Writing has indeed grown into a significant aspect of world literature. One can notice in this writing a development parallel to the multi-faceted advancement of the Indian society since Independence. What was largely a nationalistic writing during the times of Rabindranath Tagore and Sri Aurobindo has become a literature of immense aesthetic and socio-cultural significance for modern India.

According to Adil Jussawalla, Indian writing in English today

> reflects the Indian petty bourgeoisie's present inability to find a dynamic role for itself in a society which is slowly transforming itself from the semi-feudal to the capitalist. Wedged between the class that employs it and the broad masses of peasants and the growing urban proletariat, it can only torment itself with its own contradictions or turn on itself in a fury of self-destruction. This is the writing of a bourgeoisie at a dead end.[1]

Jussawalla thus sees the individual and the social contradictions embodied in the contemporary Indian writing. In fact, this writing reflects the complex state of the modern Indian society balancing itself between the capitalist and the proletariat extremes. And the Indian writers in English have generally been successful in fusing the socio-cultural values with the aesthetic, keeping pace with the intellectual currents in the

---

* *The Journal of Indian Writing in English,* VI, i (January 1978) 58-70.

outside world. With a superb mastery over the English language, these writers have evolved a distinct idiom suited to the Indian sensibility. Their language and mode of expression are no longer derivative and writing for them has become the most serious literary vocation.

Poets like Nissim Ezekiel, A.K. Ramanujan, Kamala Das, Parthasarathy, Shiv K. Kumar, Pritish Nandy, and Jayanta Mahapatra have won recognition both in India and abroad. They have improved much upon the writing of their predecessors, while consciously or unconsciously repeating certain themes and motifs common to the earlier writing. During the Sixties, Indian poetry in English recorded a distinct departure and the Seventies have shown another step in the enormous growth of the writing. Thus Ezekiel's collection of 1965, Kamala Das's *Summer in Calcutta,* A.K. Ramanujan's *The Striders,* Shiv K. Kumar's *Cobwebs in the Sun,* and R. Parthasarathy's *Rough Passage* have given a new direction to the writing of poetry in English.

According to Parthasarathy,

> Poems like 'Night of the Scorpion' and
> 'A River' by their visions of an everyday
> Indian reality expressed in an unobtrusive
> personal voice stood out in the reader's
> mind as signposts indicating the directions
> poetry in English was likely to take in
> the future.[2]

The kind of "Indian reality" that Parthasarathy finds in the contemporary Indian poetry in English is somewhat limited: it is a consciousness largely shaped by the urban life-style of the elite confined to the drawing rooms. Ezekiel's attempt at evoking the rural milieu in "Night of the Scorpion" is that of a city-dweller. While he gives expression to a very personal kind of religion, his stance is that of an ironist too. Even the major poets like Ezekiel have not entirely caught the colour of life of the millions living outside the cities. To them the average or substandard Indian is the dweller of the city slums. How about the rural folks who constitute the bulk of the Indian population? Also, in the words of the novelist Mulk Raj Anand,

> Apart from the task of seeing human relations, the permanent task of liberating the human soul in travail, the compassion necessary before affliction and pain, and the courageous conferment of one's own freedom on others, remain genuine ideals before the creative intelligentsia.[3]

Such humanistic utterances are dubbed "leftist" by the self-conscious and foppish "creative intelligentsia" to whom Anand is vainly appealing. The writings of great English poets like P.B. Shelley, Alfred Tennyson, and Matthew Arnold served as clarion calls to their contemporaries toward a new social and cultural awareness. The poetry of Rabindranath Tagore and Sri Aurobindo achieved this goal in the India of their times, carrying across the continents messages of good-will for international amity. The Indian poets writing in English today seem to be too circumscribed in their vision to present the wider "Indian reality" to the world community.

In a majority of these poets is conspicuously absent a sense of the Indian myth that brings the novels of Raja Rao and R.K. Narayan so close to the hearts of the Indian readers. In the writings of Tagore and Sri Aurobindo too, there is discernible a distinct awareness of such an Indian myth. But the contemporary poets do not generally accept the "Indianness" of the reality presented in these older poets. Thus Adil Jussawalla says:

> To my mind,...*Savitri,* a poem on the relation of the spirit to matter, unwinding like an interminable sari through twelve books and about 2400 lines is one vast onion of a poem. The layers gradually fall away to reveal nothing.[4]

Jussawalla questions a tradition which, in his view, is nothing but "a vagueness of thought, an absolute faith in the mystical, and a blind reliance in the heart." He thus fails to see the possible symbolic relevance of the mythological Savitri to the Indian womanhood. Sir Philip Sidney who in *An Apology for Poetry* maintains that the poet is superior to the philosopher, concedes that even "the philosophers of Greece durst not a long time appear to the world but under the masks of poets." Like those great philosophers of Greece, Indian poet-philosophers like Tagore and Sri Aurobindo might be conveying an idealistic view of life through poetry. The question is whether philosophy can be the subject of modern poetry.

Kamala Das's verse is often compared with the confessional poetry of Anne Sexton and Sylvia Plath. On a close reading, however, one gains the impression that her poetry is not entirely an "autobiography of a fever" of the Plath type. Sex in her poetry is often overplayed to the point of nausea and to the detriment of the hues of the salubrious familial love. Nevertheless, there seems to be a certain amount of sincerity in an occasional poem like "An Introduction." Parthasarathy, with his relatively limited bulk of writing, has established himself as one of the important poets whose style is marked by exquisite polish. Poems in *Rough Passage* reveal him as a poet of "self" in search of identity. He is generally lost in a linguistic paradox and turns to Tamil as his language of communication. Jayanta Mahapatra has written some brilliant verse. He is more authentic in the poems on Orissa than in those dealing with love, marriage, and parenthood. He occasionally deals with topical subjects in poem like "Gandhi," "The Tattooed Taste," and "The Twenty-fifth Anniversary of a Republic."

Parthasarathy's problem with language as a vehicle of poetic utterance is but a part of the larger cultural dilemma that the Indian poet in English is confronted with. In the words of A.K. Ramanujan:

> English and my disciplines (linguistics, anthropology) give me my 'outer' forms-linguistic, metrical, logical and other such ways of shaping experience; and my first thirty years in India, my frequent visits and field trips, my personal and professional preoccupations with Kannada, Tamil, the Classics and folklore give me my substance, my 'inner' forms, images and symbols. They are continuous with each other, and I no longer can tell what comes from where.[5]

In Ramanujan's poems like "Conventions of Despair" and "Prayer to Lord Murugan" a tension between "tradition" and "individual talent" is evident. And the poet at times seems to be unable to resolve that tension. This attempt at ordering experience out of the tension between "the brown skin" and

Western "bleachers" is a noteworthy feature of Shiv K. Kumar's poetry too.[6] The common charge in respect of Kumar's poetry is that he confuses sex with religion in poems like "Wife at Prayer," "To a Prostitute," and "At a Convent." The sexual fantasies in his poetry (also common to the poetry of Parthasarathy, Kamala Das, and Ezekiel) need not deter one's appreciation of the essential Kumar—'the "real Me" of Walt Whitman "with peals of distant ironical laughter"[7] at the contemporary situation. It is his superb handling of irony that gives Kumar a unique place in contemporary Indian poetry in English. Poems like "The Sun Temple of Konark" make it evident that the sexual imagery in Kumar's poetry is inspired by the erotic motifs on the Sun temple of Konark—motifs that signify a profound synthesis of the sensual and the spiritual.

While such is the brilliance of a handful of luminaries in the firmament of Indian poetry in English, their lustre is often clouded by the multiplicity of dim figures and shooting stars across the horizon. Perhaps they become more conspicuous on account of the contrasting presence of the lesser figures. The proliferation of these inferior poets has recently been attaining alarming proportions. Almost every second Indian citizen thinks that he is a poet. Particularly in the academic community, it has become a fashion to scribble some lines called "poetry" or at least to publicly exhibit one's enthusiasm for poetry. The craze of the day seems to be that an academic should concoct at least one poem before he retires.

As one enters the world of great poetry, one experiences an orchestral symphony—a symphony of the human spirit. In the words of James Joyce, all literature is "the eternal affirmation of man's spirit." The true poet, even the apparently obscurest, ultimately offers a simplification of the complexity that is life. According to Robert Frost, a real poem "ends in a clarification of life." The finest poetry, by means of its musicality—of the language as well as of the spirit—transports the reader into the realm of the Muse. The imagination of the true poet harmonizes the material and the spiritual, taking the reader beyond the immediate world of existence into the world of ideality. In the process, the reader undergoes some kind of a purge, forgetting the world of cares and anxieties. Perhaps it is for this reason that poets like T.S. Eliot, under the influence of the French symbolists, emphasized so much on the need for musicality of poetry. In the writings of the innumerable versifiers in India at the present time, one could notice not symphony of the human spirit but jarring cacophony of artificial words.

As examples of the trivial writing, one can cite lines like: "She is a mighty wench/Who held me in her trench/Kept me henpecked for long." Or, "Screams screaching we heard of men left unsheltered/Under a wild sky...." Wilder than the wildest sky! An impressive rendering of thought and feeling, which is essential to good poetry, is absent in most of these versifiers. For instance, one poet writes, "Your call/Comes to me/like a telegram/a wireless message." Another says that walking by the sea, he was "touched by the Supreme Lotion." A typical image concocted by one of these poets is worth attention: "...sun a dirty coin under/muddy water." A "muddy" image indeed! Another poet writes: "They take chicken roast with/a glass of wine. Fried grams for us...." It may be an authentic experience of the palate at a restaurant; but then a cookery book is perhaps a work of magnificent poetry.

Thus Poetry in the hands of these innumerable poetasters fails to touch the chords of the human spirit. On the contrary, it has come to be the vocation of idlers and perverted minds vainly trying to establish a symbolic connection between the Galaxy and garbage. Freedom from the constraints of the metrical form, resulting in looseness of the verse and the haphazard choice of the subject matter have made the contemporary poetry in English banal indeed. The directness of utterance, instead of being a blessing, has become a bane to much of this writing. Meenakshi Mukherji is right when she says that some of these poets are more fond of handling the English language rather than conveying a poetic vision. D.V.K. Raghavacharyulu expresses the same opinion: "A good deal of Indian poetry these days seems to be aiming at expressive strategies rather than communicative goals. Our poets purvey clippings of trendy prose as poetry...."[8] Nissim Ezekiel comes heavily on the multitude of hacks around him:

Damn all you sensitive poets
seducers of experience
. . . .
victims of your own spontaneous fraud
You are in hell
and do not know it.
When did you last write
a real poem?

A major obsession of the contemporary Indian English poets seems to be with sex. Their intention might be to depict love as a primal experience. English poets like John Donne and Robert Browning have written magnificant love poetry that at once brings out the essence of the human spirit. Much of the erotic writing of the contemporary Indian poets, on the contrary, fails to reach the level of the poetry of these British poets. Nor is it anywhere near the profound love poetry of an Indian poet like Kalidasa. Perhaps these contemporary Indian poets in English are, in their anxiety to reject the devotional, what Ben Jonson in *Valpone* calls "desperate wits."

II

In contrast to the profusion of the numbers of the poets writing in English, one notices on the Indian literary scene a limited number of fiction-writers and dramatists. What possibly is the cause for the mushroom growth of the poetasters? Is it the relaxation of the rules of the game, the prosodic form? Is fiction-writing, which requires a more sustained effort at presenting incident, character, and dialogue more difficult than writing poetry? Is presenting a passing emotion in the form of a poem easier than portraying a sustained picture of life that is the novel? Do emotional upheavals, supposed to be a major contributing factor for the birth of the creative faculty, order themselves more easily into poetry than into the creation of a panorama of fictional world which stimulates the reader, making him more alive?

The "Indian reality" that Parthasarathy finds in the poetry of Ezekiel is presented in greater detail in the works of the novelists and short-story writers. Raja Rao depicts the situation of the individual in India in the metaphysical context. R.K. Narayan, with his subtle comic sense, evokes the unique atmosphere of Malgudi in his fiction. Mulk Raj Anand focuses attention on the suffering millions of India—the Bakhas of his fictional world. Bhabani Bhattacharya exposes the deceptions of the pious in the Indian society. Kamala Markandaya tries to resolve the tension between tradition and modernity, East and West, the rural and the urban.

Vasant A. Shahane says:

> The Indo-Anglian novel is in many ways a haphazard growth and its fortuitous development is partly the product of lack of clear objectives. An objective like the image of India or Western reader is more often a pious platitude than a genuinely realized artistic goal.[9]

One has only to read the novels and short-stories of the authors mentioned above to see the "image of India" presented in all its significance for the Indian and the Western reader. The three major novelists Raja Rao, R.K. Narayan, and Mulk Raj Anand together have remarkably succeeded in depicting India in both the spiritual and socio-cultural aspects. Anand's experiments in technique are well-known. It is surprising that while mentioning even Manohar Malagaonkar and Kamala Markandaya as "novelists of front rank," Shahane does not care to refer to the humanist even once in the whole essay. What has been marring an accurate evaluation of the Indian novelists in English is perhaps such a critical myopia. Shahane further says:

> Literary critics in their enthusiasm to win recognition for the identity of Indo-Anglian fiction have fallen an easy prey to the temptation of overrating these authors, especially novelists. In retrospect, this seems to me an avoidable critical aberration.[10]

It is necessary to refer in this connection to a painstaking study of a clumsy journalistic writer like Khushwant Singh done by Shahane himself, reading into his work a basic mythical pattern and symbolic mode. Meenakshi Mukherjee finds "myth" in the Indian English novel as a structural device. While she sees such a "myth" in the works of Raja Rao and R.K. Narayan, she questions Mulk Raj Anand for the absence of it. By her own admission, however "Anand was at the height of his power in the 'thirties' and early 'forties,' when a sociological approach to literature was very much in vogue in India as well as outside."[11] Even today Anand continues to write in the same sociological vein for which he was so famous three decades ago. And the significance of his work for the future generation lies in the fact that he has evolved a "new myth" of the contemporary human predicament.

Taken together, the writings of the Indian English novelists cover a vaster area of the Indian reality than those of the poets. The chief interest of the novel, as Northrop Frye puts it, is in "human character as it manifests itself in society." The "human character" in India is extremely complex on account of the diversity of the Indian culture. The writings of the leading novelists like Raja Rao, R.K. Narayan, Mulk Raj Anand, Kamala Markandaya, and Manohar Malgaonkar, in spite of their "Indianness" in the larger sense of the term, are restricted to certain regional cultures. There are still too many aspects of the Indian life yet to be highlighted by the Indian-English writers. Novelists and short-story writers in the regional languages have no doubt written at great length about these multiple regional and sub-regional cultures. The need of the hour seems to be a proliferation of fiction-writers to depict all the diversity and variety of the Indian life. Fiction, on account of the very expansive nature of the genre, is capable of presenting a sustained picture of life.

III

Ever since the appearance of Rabindranath Tagore's plays like *The King and the Queen, Sacrifice,* and *Malini* with their shadowy ideas, T.P. Kailasam's *Burden, Fulfilment,* and *Karna* with their Puranic themes, and Bharati Sarabhai's pageants like *The Welt of the People* and *Two Women,* Indian dramatic writing in English has not been impressive either quantitatively or qualitatively. There is of course an isolated play like Girish Karnad's *Tughlaq* or Shanta Rama Rao's adaptation of Forster's *A Passage to India* or, more recently, Shiv K. Kumar's *The Last Wedding Anniversary* giving an unfulfilled promise for a systematic writing of plays in English by Indians. Nissim Ezekiel's three plays, *Nalini, Marriage Poem* and *The Sleepwalkers* are comedies and farces that fail to produce a lasting impression on the theatre-goers. Perhaps these plays are more convincing in Marathi than in English. Ezekiel's attempts at dramatic writing in English remind us of the colossal failure of English poets like Robert Browning at the theatre. Asif Currimbhoy emerges as the best contemporary Indian playwright in English. Fubin Bowers is convincing when he maintains that Currimbhoy's plays reveal him to be India's first authentic voice in the theatre.[12] Currimbhoy says that the essence of theatre is conflict.[13] In fact, conflict is the essence of the Western theatre since Euripedes and Sophocles. Currimbhoy's plays like *Goa, Sonar Bangla,* and *Inquilab* deal with themes of wide topical interest and the central conflict in them, presented in an authentic language, arises from the juxtaposition of the public event with the private experience of the character.

In spite of the comparative success of Currimbhoy, Indian dramatic writing in English continues to be immature. K.R. Srinivasa Iyengar is convincing when he says:

> The paucity of good actable English dramas written by Indians is mainly attributable to the fact that the natural medium of conversation with us...excepting for the supersophisticated who live in the cities and the larger towns, in the Universities or in certain Government offices or business houses—is the mother tongue rather than English, and hence, unless the characters and situations are carefully chosen, it would be difficult to make a dialogue between Indians in English sound convincing.[14]

Thus the dichotomy between the spoken language and atmosphere may be responsible for the failure of Indian drama in English. Another factor may be the absence of the element of make-believe which is essential to the success of drama. Hence a play like Ezekiel's *Marriage Poem* is more successful in Marathi than in English. The audiences that turn up for these plays in English are the educated and the cultivated. Even then, on account of the transfer of an unfamiliar foreign atmosphere to the stage, the Indian audiences fail to get totally involved in the spectacle before them. The imaginative re-creation of life that is essential for the element of make-believe is absent and hence there is a communication gap between the dramatist and the audience. Under these circumstances, the "Indian reality" that these dramatists writing in English try to present becomes unreal and unconvincing. The difficulties in the way of the Indian playwrights in English may be overcome if they employ the kind of English spoken in India—English filled with Indianisms.

IV

We have thus briefly surveyed the Indian English literary scene wherein the novelists and playwrights look like purple patches on a landscape covered with innumerable poets and poetasters. If Indian life is to be adequately presented to the outside world, there should be a proportionate growth of the fiction-writers and dramatists. The poets themselves should probe into the real reality around them in all its aspects. Very few Indian poets are concerned with the exquisite Indian flora and fauna to the extent they should have been. As a result we have yet to see a Wordsworth or a Frost among our Indian English poets. In addition, our poets normally confine themselves to a depiction of the urban sensibility, spurning both the kind of life that Mulk Raj Anand describes and the one that Rabindranath Tagore or Sri Aurobindo describes.

While writing in English, some of our novelists and poets try to evoke the specifically occidental. In spite of all their "Indianness," perhaps they cannot avoid the formidable Western influence not only because the language of their expression is English but because they continue to derive consciously or unconsciously from the Western methods of composition. Just as in life, in literature too, more and more Indians are now looking in the direction of the United States of America for models. Hence, it may not be improper to suggest that the phrase "Indian American Writing" may be used in the place of "Indian English Writing" in specific instances. The profound influence of the American language, life, and culture on the contemporary Indian writers in English may thus be worth a close study. Shiv K. Kumar's admiration for contemporary American poetry is well-known. Despite his initial experimentation on the basis of his British experience, Nissim Ezekiel often turns his attention to the American writers. Having been an expatriate living in Chicago, A.K. Ramanujan cannot escape the impact. While a few novelists like Kamala Markandaya, living in England, continue to re-create the Indian

English sensibility, others like Raja Rao and R.K. Narayan have turned toward the New World. These poets and novelists may not be consciously copying anything American; but the indirect (however limited) influence cannot be ruled out on account of their intense admiration for the American genius.

In addition to all these factors, publishing industry and critical reception also influence the direction that the contemporary Indian English writing takes. The enormous growth of substandard poetry can be attributed to the fact that the editors of magazines find it more convenient to include a poem than a short story for reasons of space. Very few popular journals publish novels in serial form. This serialization is very much in vogue in the Indian language journals. One can notice more poetasters represented in popular magazines like. *The Illustrated Weekly of India* than fiction-writers and dramatists. Of course *Enact* is doing a good job in regularly publishing plays in English by Indians and one occasionally comes across an interesting piece. Editors like P. Lal are doing a great service to the cause of Indian English writing by publishing collections of poems and even full-length novels. But the quality of these publications has yet to improve. Even in *The Journal of Indian Writing in English,* one finds more poetry than fiction or drama. M. Sivaramakrishna complains against "the subtle publishing and promotional maneouvres" of the poets, saying:

> These have wide-spread tentacles reaching to such an extent that many poets personally edit articles on their own poetry or cleverly get articles, reviews and books commissioned for known supporters.[15]

These words of an experienced critic of Indian English writing are worth attention. They throw considerable light on much of the present-day criticism of Indian English writing. If a poet edits articles or reviews on his own poetry done by a friend or a sycophant, it is because of an anxiety common to all creative writers the world over to see that they are not misrepresented. The fault in such cases is not the poet's but the sycophant's, because the latter does the assignment to please the writer, thereby expecting some benefits. One often comes across such "hypocritical" scholars in academic departments. These criticasters are like the rope-dancers in

Gulliver's Travels who break their bones to please the man in power, expecting professional survival or advancement. They start throwing missiles at the very men whom they had eulogized, if they fail to get the reward expected. Sincerity and candour, two of the important qualities that Alexander Pope prescribes for the ideal critic in *An Essay on Criticism,* are also essential for criticasters who write "commissioned" articles or reviews for some patron, poet or novelist. Once this situation improves, Indian English writers get what is due to them from their critics.

NOTES

1. Adil Jussawalla, *New Writing in India* (New Delhi: Penguin Books, 1974) 34.
2. R. Parthasarathy, "How it Strikes a Contemporary: The Poetry of A.K. Ramanujan," *The Literary Criterion* (Special Number on Indian Writing in English), XII, Nos. 2-3 (1976) 188.
3. Mulk Raj Anand, "Trends in the Modern Indian Novel," *The Journal of Indian Writing in English,* I, (January, 1973) 5.
4. Adil Jussawalla, "The New Poetry," *Readings in Commonwealth Literature,* ed. William Walsh (Oxford, 1973) 76.
5. R. Parthasarathy, ed., *Ten Twentieth-Century Indian Poets* (New Delhi, 1976) 95-96.
6. Shiv K. Kumar, "A Letter from New York," *Subterfuges* (New Delhi, 1976) 22.
7. Walt Whitman, "As I Ebb'd with the Ocean of Life," *Walt Whitman: Representative Selections,* ed. Floyd Stovall (New York, 1934) 183.
8. Review of A. Viswam's *River My Guru, The Journal of Indian Writing in English,* II, ii (July, 1974) 65.
9. Vasant A. Shahane, "Indo-English Fiction and the Question of Form," *The Journal of Indian Writing in English,* II, ii (July, 1974) 35.
10. *Ibid.*
11. Meenakshi Mukherji, *The Twice-Born Fiction* (New Delhi, 1971) 78.
12. Fubin Bowers, "Introduction," *Asif Currimbhoy's Plays* (New Delhi, 1972).
13. *"Commentary* meets Asif Currimbhoy," *Commentary* (Journal of the University of Singapore Society), ed. Pauline Baratham & Kirpal Singh, I, iii (February, 1976) 42.
14. K.R. Srinivasa Iyengar, *Indian Writing in English* (Bombay, 1962) 197.
15. M. Sivaramakrishna, "The 'Tongue in English Chains' Indo-English Poetry Today," *Osmania Journal of English Studies* (Contemporary Indian Poetry in English Special Number), XIII, i (1977) 219.

5

MULTICULTURALISM AND INDIAN (ENGLISH) LITERATURE*

Contemporary Indian culture is extremely complex and fascinating on account of the peculiar amalgam of tradition and modernity, as well as the multiplicity of subcultures and languages. The literary works, either in the regional languages or in English, are a significant means of communicating the vast variety and diversity of such a culture. While the treasures of regional literatures remain largely hidden from the sight of even Indians belonging to diverse regions, Indian English literature is somewhat limited in scope, dealing with certain common cultural traits. Indian language writers as well as Indian English writers have yet to probe deeper into the submerged layers of their own cultures.

I

Referring to the situation faced by the serious Indian novelist after Independence, K.R. Srinivasa Iyengar says:

> The old narrow loyalties were seen to wax as eloquent as ever. Communal, linguistic, casteist passions were seen to come into the open with accelerated frequency. While talk of "emotional integration" filled the air, the *terra ferma* only witnessed the agonizing spectacle of a divided house with a deceptive floor and a precarious roof. It required the shock therapy of brutal aggression by the Chinese in October-November 1962 and by Pakistan in September 1965 to forge in the mass consciousness a new sense of unity and urgency and a stern common

* LITTCRIT (Trivandrum), Vol. 17, No. 1 & 2, June-Dec. 1991, 12-22.

> purpose reminiscent of the peak moments of the Gandhian age. But the moment the external pressure relaxed, the mood passed too, and once again the winds of disunity and purposelessness began to blow again.[1]

This state of the Indian society may persist even today, but there is no cause for alarm since there are checks and balances inherent in the Indian system. The Indian multiculturalism should not be viewed in the narrow perspective of what the newspapers call "fissiparous tendencies." The common factors of "Indianness" notwithstanding, each of the subcultures presents a unique value system. It is essential to be aware of the multiple subcultures so that we feel reassured of the richness of Indian life. These various local cultures are but the warp and woof of the overall fabric of Indian society. As a vibrant society, India has undergone great changes over the centuries. But the uniqueness of Indian culture lies in its flexibility, the overall structure remaining ever strong despite upheavals.

Krishna Kripalani focuses on the multiplicity of Indian languages and says:

> Such then is the linguistic jigsaw puzzle of modern India. Without a proper appreciation of this complex pattern one is likely to miss the significance of one of the most characteristic aspects of modern Indian literature, namely, its multiple character. It has been said that Indian literature is one, though written in many languages—a faint echo of the famous Vedic verse: "Truth is one though sages call it by various names." This characteristic permeates not only literature but almost every significant aspect of Indian culture. Hence, the hackneyed phrase, "Unity in Diversity," which our politicians and culture mongers are never tired of repeating, although there is at least as much diversity in our unity as there is unity in our diversity.[2]

On account of the "complex pattern" of Indian life, its various geographical areas, the Indian languages and literatures too have a multiple character. It is true that the overall temperate climate of the country has given the Indians an apparently common outlook and temperament moulding their thought and action. The intellectual and cultural movements in India were inspired by religious motives, but the impact of Western culture on the educated class has served as a unifying factor. This is all the more on account of the absence of a link language. English language and Westernized life style have indeed served as a common bond among the Indian elitist circles. But the elite constitute a small percentage of the Indian population. Abid Hussain admits that "the search for, and love of unity, was sometimes carried to such extremes as to altogether deny the reality of the manifold phenomena which make up the physical world."[3] He expresses an apprehension that in view of the "centrifugal forces" at work, "the country might face cultural disintegration, leading first to political anarchy and then to foreign domination."[4] Whatever the political aspects of such an apprehension, it is baseless in terms of culture. There will be no "cultural disintegration" of India if its multiple cultures are allowed to flourish. In fact, the combination of these multiple cultures only brings to light the essential richness of the Indian society. As A.L. Basham asserts:

> The Indian tradition of a hierarchically graded society may yet survive, but in a form rather different from the traditional caste system. The intense feeling of kinship which seems common to almost all Indians, whatever their religion, may persist even after the break up of the joint family.[5]

On account of economic competition and Westernization, the joint family system in India is breaking up and the system of a "hierarchically graded society" remains ever strong. In the words of M.N. Srinivas, "Each caste has a culture which is to some extent autonomous: there are differences in dress, speech, manners, ritual and ways of life."[6] Whatever their public stance, even the educated elite privately adhere to the practices of their particular castes.

Indian culture does not consist of only Maharajahs, elephants, and snake charmers on the social level and Maya, Karma and Advaita on the spiritual. In the contemporary situation, it has changed immensely. While the ancient Indian tradition is a source of great strength for the Indian mind, it is the ever-changing contemporary hi-tech culture that contributes to the advancement of the society. The simultaneous presence of tradition and modernity makes Indian culture unique today. But we should also be aware of the much hypocrisy and double standard that have characterized the modern educated elite, largely the negative effect of Westernization. Perhaps this is a sort of biculturation!

A society consists of individuals, organized and interacting. As S.F. Nadel puts it, "Society, as I see it, means the totality of social facts projected on to the dimension of relationships and groupings; culture, the same totality in the dimension of action."[7] Culture is generally known as the socially sanctioned behaviour of a people. It is a way of life of a people. One of the best early definitions of culture was given by E.B. Tylor, who described it as "that complex whole which includes knowledge, belief, art, morals, law, custom and any other capabilities and habits acquired by man as a member of society."[8] Culture includes all the endowments acquired by man from his group by both conscious learning and unconscious conditioning process. The individual learns the values of his society through a process of enculturation.

Cultural anthropologists acknowledge particularities in specific cultures despite the universals. According to Melville J. Herskovits, culture is "a series of limits within which the behaviour and ideas of the members of a given society may exhibit approved differences. In the larger view, these differences are to be regarded as setting the boundaries of sanctioned variation."[9] Thus, there will certainly be "approved differences" among the members of a particular culture. Herskovits also maintains that "no two cultures are the same."[10]

The mosaic of subcultures constituting the United States of America has given rise to the concept of "Cultural Pluralism." America as a nation of nations is known for its multiple streams of immigrant groups. The "Melting Pot" of the American society, greatly eulogized by Crevecoeur, is in fact a myth. Indian sociologists acknowledge the numerous groups of immigrants from different parts of Asia and Europe—the Negrito, the Proto-Australoid, the Mongoloid, the Mediterranean, the Western Brachycephals, and the Nordic—settled down in India, but the culture of each group has undergone enough change over the centuries to become an integral part of the Indian mosaic.[11] While the presence of subcultures in India may not be an exact parallel to the American situation, there are nevertheless variations in India resulting from the impact of Muslim and Christian cultures in addition to the ancient racial settlements. Referring to the American situation, Andrew T. Kopan says that "a distinctive set of values is nurtured in the social groupings defined by religious affiliation."[12] Perhaps this cultural variation is present in India too where multiple religions exist, often determining the course of social life. The variety of the Indian culture is more palpable in the sub-regional cultures even within the individual linguistic groups in several states of the country. But all these multicultural variations have only contributed to the richness and colour of Indian culture. The subcultural groups are sometimes called "deviant cultural groups."

The contemporary society has a mass culture in which most people think and believe alike. They read the same type of books and journals and enjoy the same type of entertainment like cinema and T.V. On account of the world-wide spread of higher technology, this kind of mass culture is conspicuous in Indian society too. Another significant aspect of the contemporary Indian culture is the presence of a deviant cultural group called the elite. The educated elite constituting a minority are a distinct group in addition to the majority poor as well as the lesser numbers of the middle and lower middle classes.

II

Commenting on the present-day Indian movies, the *Washington Post* has said recently: "Indian films rarely reflect the vast diversity of Indian society. All of them seem to occur in the same village, in the same street, in the same town or a rich man's mansion."[13] This limited and stereotyped presentation of Indian culture is conspicuous in Indian English literature. Even though the novelists and poets writing in English belong to various cultural groups, and in spite of certain variations of settings, they generally tend to present the same stereotyped themes like the East-West encounter, the rural-urban conflict, and Vedantic mysticism. Whether on account of a foreign medium of expression or Westernization on the part of the Indian English writer resulting in lack of total involvement with the Indian situation, the imaginative writings sound inadequate in representing the multi-faceted Indian culture.

Creative writing in Indian languages is extremely vast and complex, reflecting not only the Indian culture in its broad features, but also in the several regional and sub-regional aspects. However, while popular and cheap writings proliferate, one feels that something more serious can still be said in Indian languages to bring out the cultural variety. In spite of the enormity of the literatures in Indian languages, it is difficult to have access to the writings in languages other than one's own. Authentic translations of regional fiction and poetry into English may help us appreciate the other Indian subcultures. The rituals, folklore, and social customs of one region vastly differ from those of the others. But this richness of the Indian cultural tapestry is not known even to the majority of Indians, not to speak of the foreigners.

In a recent article, Reed Way Dasenbrock uses the term "multicultural literature" to include "both works that are explicitly about multicultural societies and those that are implicitly multicultural in the sense of inscribing readers from other cultures inside their own textual dynamics."[14] Thus, a literature like the Indian English not only presents the multiple Indian cultural scene but also poses problems of reader-response for those belonging to the other cultures, universality notwithstanding. The Indian multiculturalism refers to the multistate, multicommunal, multilingual Indian nation as a whole. Some aspects of this national multiculturalism—*e.g.*, the multiculturalism of religious communities like Jain, Shiaite Muslim, Syrian Christian, and Parsi in different Hindu-dominated states or the English-speaking multilinguals like the Gujaratis, the Punjabis, the Tamils and the Malayalees dispersed in different regions outside their own native places—are not cross-cultural. Multiculturalism also means the complexity, if not duality, in Indian individuals, prevalent among English-users as well as among other bi- and multi-linguals. However, the most isolated mono-cultured villager out of touch with the modern society presents an interesting case study. Indian English writers, novelists as well as poets generally, tend to be ironic in presenting such a mono-cultured

Indian villager, may be on account of their distance from him resulting from their own pseudo-Western urban upbringing. Total involvement on the part of the writer and a sympathetic rendering of the typically Indian cultural or subcultural scene is more conspicuous in literatures written in Indian languages.

Mulk Raj Anand in his novels and short stories depicts the lives of poor and suffering masses. And his works have a typically Punjabi flavor. R.K. Narayan presents the South Indian small town man, more specifically the Kannadiga. While Raja Rao escapes into the realm of Maya following disillusionment on account of East-West encounter, Bhabani Bhattacharya exposes the hypocrisy of religious practitioners in India and in the West. The rural-urban conflict presented in the novels of Kamala Markandaya sometimes sounds like the perspective of an outsider. Nayantara Sahgal deals with the lives of politicians and fashionable pseudo-Western upper-class Indians lost in the cultural limbo. Manohar Malgaonkar deals with the lives of the fossilized princes and princesses. All these major novelists have, of course, dealt with some segments of Indian society. But there are many more aspects that do not appear in these writings. Among the contemporary Indian English poets, Nissim Ezekiel evokes the specifically urban climate. A.K. Ramanujan presents the South Indian customs and beliefs in subtle poetic terms. Jayanta Mahapatra's poetry transports us into the culture of Orissa. However, as Balachandra Rajan puts it, it is impossible to expect from these poets "to assist in forging a national image or to contribute to a national myth."[15] Rajan's dissatisfaction with Indian English poetry is understandable since it is limited in range and depth. In fact, the Indian English novelists have dealt with a relatively wider range of Indian life and culture. However, the literary forms and traditions in Indian languages are richer and more complex than in Indian English poetry and fiction. When Indians write in English, they try to look thoroughly "English," not "Indian English," and they use Western forms and imitate Western feelings to cater to the audiences in the West as well as to the elitist educated circles in India. There is no genuine attempt at reaching the average English-knowing Indian readers who constitute yet another deviant cultural group.

Traditionalism alone is not "Indian" today, since most educated Indians, including Indian English writers and their critics, are not really acquainted with the profundities and complexities of Indian tradition. Break up of the joint family and urbanization have caused great changes in Indian society. Without an in-depth knowledge of the multiple local cultures, these writers are often torn between Indian sensibility and pseudo-Westernization. In India, as in America, consumer culture is growing, and the higher technology is making itself manifest even in rural life. The Indian English writers cannot avoid this aspect of contemporary Indian life.

The East-West encounter as a theme in Indian English literature has become a stereotype. What the Indian English writer should present is not his own "encounter" with the West but the gradual change that is coming over the Indian society on account of hi-tech culture. Americans are homogenized by mass mediated consumer culture, in spite of the ethnicity of their society. In India, the homogenization by mass mediated consumer culture may not be taking place to the extent it is in America, but the change in the Indian life style is evident. There is significant change in the younger generation. In fact, even the older generation today is getting adjusted to the newer modes of living. A sort of liberated and uninhibited attitude can be seen among some sections of the urban elite. Nevertheless, the majority still look back to the tradition. So the paradox of the Indian mind persists.

Another conspicuous level of Indian multiculturalism prevailing today is that of the critics of Indian English literature. As Balachandra Rajan laments, "Much criticism of contemporary Indian writing still consists of the ill-concealed airing of private feuds."[16] The reason for such a state of affairs is the control exercised by Indian academics on the critical scene. Some of the academics themselves are writers and they sell their wares by using their academic positions. The critics of Indian English literature have to support their hopes of academic promotions. Just as the cultural or cross-cultural backgrounds of the Indian English writers are diverse, so also those of the Indian readers. Sometimes the academic readers may tend to be cleverer, more pseudo-Western and opportunistic than the writers themselves!

The regional literatures in India have cultural histories very different from that of Indian English literature. If the cultural history of Indian English literature is more limited than that of any regional Indian literature, it is different too from that of the Christian literature of the West. The Indian English writers have yet to rediscover their own roots and present the various regional cultures in all their depth and variety. And Indian critics should write more about culturally related areas. Generally they are acquainted with only part of their own particular cultures. Most of them are not acquainted with the other regional cultures. Popularization of authentic English translations of works of culture and creative writings of various regions may help critics attempt inter-cultural interpretations. They are generally Eurocentric in bias. Perhaps such comparisons are inevitable since the Indian critics, largely academics, are either educated in the West or even in Indian universities, their curriculum is largely Western in bias. Also since the Indian writers in English have themselves some Western background, cross-culturality is perhaps inevitable. The Indian culture today is an amalgam of the two traditions—the Hindu-Brahmanical, and the Leavisite-Eliotism; the Hindu myths and social protests and higher technology of New India. Both in Indian English literature and its criticism one finds this paradoxical combination. Perhaps multiculturalism is inevitable in the Indian literary situation, as in the social context.

NOTES

1. K.R. Srinivasa Iyengar, *Indian Writing in English* (1962; rpt. New Delhi: Sterling Publishing Pvt. Ltd., 1984) 320.
2. Krishna Kripalani, "Modern Literature," in *A Cultural History of India*, ed. A.L. Basham (1975; rpt. Delhi: Oxford University Press, 1987) 407.
3. A. Abid Hussain, *The National Culture of India* (1956; rpt. New Delhi: National Book Trust, 1987) 18.
4. *Ibid.*, 168.
5. A.L. Basham 498.
6. M.N. Srinivas, *India: Social Structure* (1969; rpt. Delhi: Hindustan Publishing Corporation, 1986) 11.
7. S.F. Nadel, *The Foundations of Social Anthropology* (London, 1951) 79-80.

8. E.B. Tylor, *Primitive Culture* (New York, 1874) I, 1.
9. Melville J. Herskovits, *Cultural Relativism: Perspectives in Cultural Pluralism,* ed. Frances Herskovits (New York: Random House, 1972) 247.
10. Melville J. Herskovits, *Cultural Anthropology* (New York: Alfred A. Knopf, 1958) 307.
11. *See* M.N. Srinivas 1.
12. Andrew Kopan, "Melting Pot: Myth or Reality," in *Cultural Pluralism,* ed. Edgar G. Epps (Berkeley: McCutcheon Publishing Corporation, 1974) 53.
13. Quoted in *Indian Express,* October 27, 1988.
14. Reed Way Dasenbrock, "Intelligibility and Meaningfulness in Multicultural Literature in English," *PMLA,* Vol. 102, No. 1 (January 1987) 10.
15. Balachandra Rajan, "India," in *Literatures of the World in English,* ed. Bruce King (London: Routledge and Kegan Paul, 1974) 94.
16. *Ibid.,* 97.

6

INDIAN ENGLISH PROSE WRITING*

Ever since the publication of V.K. Gokak's *The Golden Treasury of Indo-Anglian Poetry,* quite a few anthologies of Indian poetry in English have appeared on the literary scene. But the wider field of English prose written by Indians since the first decade of the nineteenth century is as yet an un-tilled domain to many readers. The present essay aims to help the modern reader to gain a proper perspective concerning the way in which English prose in India has evolved. The enthusiastic reader will thus be able to discover treasures for himself while turning up the soil of this vast territory.

Indian poetry in English has been somewhat limited in scope in spite of more than a century of its own existence. But prose writing has flourished, reflecting the essential aspects of the Indian mind and presenting the multiplicity of moods and changes in a kaleidoscopic manner.

I

Prose writing in English in India came earlier than versification on account of the circumstances prevailing during British rule. As a subject race Indians found themselves compelled to communicate with their masters in the foreign tongue. Even before the British introduced English education in the country, there was steadily growing an English-based class of Indians constituting the elite of the society. On account of Western impact resulting in study of English literature and European thought, there was a new awakening in the Indian consciousness and a new mode of expression.

* *Indian English Prose: An Anthology* ed. D. Ramakrishna (New Delhi: Arnold-Heinemann, 1980) 11-19.

Raja Rammohan Roy was one of the earliest to plead for English education in India even before Macaulay wrote his Minute. While Rammohan Roy's tract on *sati* appeared in 1818, even much earlier, the Kavali brothers, Venkata Ramaswamy, Venkata Lakshmaiah, and Venkata Boraiah wrote English prose. Venkata Boraiah's dissertation on the Jains was published in the *Journal of the Royal Asiatic Society* in 1801.[1]

After the inauguration of the Indian National Congress in 1885 and the major universities in the nineteenth century, the use of English in India took a different turn, permeating into the very structure of the society. The leading personalities in the Congress used English prose in their attempts to convince the rulers about the need for Indian independence. However, by 1890, the eulogistic tone of the previous decade gave place to patriotic utterance in a prose charged with emotion.

About this time the religious reform movements like Brahmo Samaj, Arya Samaj, and Prarthana Samaj ushered in a new spiritual awakening in the country. Under the influence of Sri Ramakrishna Paramhamsa, Keshub Chander Sen wanted Indians to come out of their Iethargy and Swami Vivekananda with his global sweep, brought India face to face with Western civilization. There was a considerable amount of prose writing by these religious and social reformers.

The writings of the pioneers like Mahadeo Govind Ranade, K.T. Telang, Surendranath Banerjee, Rash Behari Ghose, Bal Gangadhar Tilak, Sri Aurobindo, Gopal Krishna Gokhale, and Lala Lajpat Rai would reveal a high degree of scholarship and personal integrity in addition to their skilful handling of the English language. What is perhaps unacceptable to the modern reader in their writings is their ornate style marred by tautology. Subsequently, however, in the writings of Gandhi, V.S. Srinivasa Sastri, Rajagopalachari and Dr Radhakrishnan, one finds a refreshing change for a flexible style. When the writer tends to use language to express his inmost thoughts and feelings, his style takes on a delightfully personal note. Some of the best non-fictional prose writers in this category are Jawaharlal Nehru, K.R. Srinivasa Iyengar, K.M. Paniker, Nirad C. Chaudhuri, Khushwant Singh, Nissim Ezekiel, M.C.

Chagla, and K.P.S. Menon. These writers have successfully rendered in a felicitous prose the complexity of the Indian culture.

Of particular significance to the student of English prose by Indians are the writings of Dom Moraes and Ved Mahta who have written about Indian culture from an alienated Western point of view. There is about their writings a certain grace and urbanity that make them delightful to read.

Another class of non-fictional prose writers is constituted by the professional journalists like C.Y. Chintamani, K. Natarajan, Khasa Subba Rao, S. Mulgoakar, V.K. Narasimhan, N. Raghunathan, M. Chalapati Rau, Chanchal Sarkar, D.R. Mankekar and Kuldip Nayar. Journalism, generally taken to mean thinness of intellectual and emotional content, has become in their hands a branch of writing noted for prophetic vision.

II

The term "Indo-Anglian" and "Indo-English" had been employed for some time to designate the writing in English by Indians. But, more recently, the term "Indian English" has been gaining currency in academic circles. What was once used in a derogatory sense signifying ungrammatical usage and inadequate grasp of the English idiom, ("Indian English") has come to be accepted widely as meaning "English in India." It is different from the mother-tongue varieties like British English, American English, Canadian English or Australian English. The language that Indians use is conditioned by certain cultural factors within the geographical bounds of India. The role of culture as a determinant in the evolution of language has been stressed by linguists. Thus J.J. Gumperz says:

> An Indian may speak English with near-native control; he may read it, write it and lecture in it with great success. But when he uses English in India his speech will share many of the features of the other Indian codes with which English alternates in the daily round of activities. Indian English will thus deviate considerably from the norms current among native speakers of English in the American Midwest. This kind of deviation represents not a failure to control English, but a natural consequence of the social

> conditions in the immediate environment in which Indian English is spoken.[2]

Depending upon the changing times and variations in local cultures, there are a number of standard Englishes even among the English-speaking countries. These variations are possible in India too, being one of the former British colonies. According to M.A.K. Halliday:

> The most important development of all is seen in the emergence of varieties of English that are identified with and specific to particular countries from among the former British colonies.[3]

Thus the structure of the particular society in which English is used causes, in course of time, a certain local standard. This localisation results in several "Indian-English" styles consequent upon the variations in regional cultures, notwithstanding the common Indian features. However, "Indian English" does not mean a mixture of English and Indian languages. Certain words like "colony," "compound," "almirah," and "prepone" are either local variations or specific only to India. This happens because the meaning of words is determined by the socio-cultural contexts in which they are used. According to Shivendra K. Verma, the Indianness of Indian English,

> lies in the fact that, within the overall general framework of the systems of English, it displays certain distinguishing phonological, lexico-semantic, and also syntactic features. In terms of linguistic efficiency these patterns are as good as any other. They are not corrupt, but different forms of the same language.[4]

The levels at which English in India is used are two: the general use of the language by various people in day-to-day life and the creative writer's use of it. The creative writer himself uses the language at two levels : when he speaks in his own voice and when he makes his characters speak in theirs. On the whole, as Shivendra K. Verma asserts, English in India

> is used as a vehicle of Indian culture to express culturally determined networks of activities that are typically Indian; for example, the social stratification of India, the caste

> systems, and a complex network of personal and societal faiths and beliefs.[5]

When the non-fictional prose writer, like the creative artist, has to convey specifically Indian thoughts and feelings he may tend to use a kind of English that is peculiar to his situation. Thus the main problem before the Indian writer in English is to convey the specifically Indian feelings and thought processes in a foreign medium.

As Raja Rao says in his Foreword to *Kanthapura*:

> One has to convey in a language that is not one's own the spirit that is one's own. One has to convey the various shades and omissions of a certain thought-movement that looks maltreated in an alien language. I use the word "alien," yet English is not really an alien language to us. It is the language of our intellectual make-up—like Sanskrit or Persian was before—but not of our emotional make-up. We are all instinctively bilingual, many of us writing in our own language and in English. We cannot write like the English. We should not. We cannot write only as Indians. We have grown to look at the large world as part of us. Our method of expression, therefore, has to be a dialect which will some day prove to be as distinctive and colourful as the Irish or the American. Time alone will justify it.

Prophetic as the words of Raja Rao are, Indian English, like the American English, Australian English, Canadian English or Irish English, has been gradually acquiring a respectable status of its own as a dialect of English acceptable to the international community.

According to R.K. Narayan,

> So far English has had a comparatively confined existence in our country, chiefly in the halls of learning, justice, or administration. Now the time is ripe for it to come to the dusty street, market place, and under the banyan tree. English must adopt the complexion of our life and assimilate its idiom. I am not suggesting here a mongrelisation of the language. I am not recommending that we should go back to the days when we heard, particularly in the railway, "Wer U go in,' man?" Bharat English will respect the rule

> of law and maintain the dignity of grammar, but still have a Swadeshi stamp about it unmistakably, like the Madras handloom check shirt or the Thirupathi doll.[6]

Narayan himself uses English in such a sophisticated way as to evoke a particularly Indian atmosphere without degenerating into linguistic absurdities.

The users of English in India are English-based bilinguals whose language interacts with Indian languages and Indian culture. The result is an unavoidable Indian flavour of some degree or the other. Mulk Raj Anand goes a step further when he tries to naturalize the alien language by literal translation or Hindi or Punjabi idiom into English. As he says:

> I generally translate or interpret my feelings or thoughts from Punjabi or Hindustani into the English language, thus translating the metaphor or imagery of my mother tongue into what is called Indo-Anglo-Indian writing, but what I prefer to call 'pigeon-Indian.' (not Pidgin-Indian)[7]

The sentiments expressed by Raja Rao and R.K. Narayan are echoed in the words of Anand:

> ...even when Indians know English grammar and have been used to speaking the alien language for a long time, they tend to feel and think in their own mother tongues. And often, the native speech enters into the shell of the sentence in the foreign language through certain indigenous words.[8]

In fact, Raja Rao has gone to the extent of saying that we cannot and should not write like the Englishmen because English is the language of our intellectual make-up but not of our emotional make-up.

III

While non-fictional prose in English had existed in abundance since the first decade of the nineteenth century, it was only in the 1920s that Indian English fiction became a popular literary form. Before 1920, however, there were a few novels like Bankim Chandra Chatterjee's *Raj Mohan's Wife* (1864), Sarath Kumar Ghose's *The Prince of Destiny* (1909), S.N. Mitra's *Hindupur* (1909), and T. Ramakrishnan's *The Dive for Death: An Indian Romance* (1911). But K.S. Venkataramani's

Murugan the Tiller (1927) is generally taken as the first representative Indian English novel. Having thus taken on a definite shape in the 1920s Indian English novel recorded a steady growth during the next two decades. Subsequently in the 1960s and 70s, it has attained a preeminent position in English fiction in the world at large, keeping pace with the changing tendencies in theme and technique. The short story form has been tried by almost all the novelists.

Some of the earliest novels like S.N. Mitra's *Hindupur* and S.K. Ghose's *The Prince of Destiny* were historical romances. In the 1930s and 40s, the Indian English novel dealt with nationalistic themes, depicting the newly emerging social and political consciousness in the country. As years advanced, novelists began dealing with significant aspects of Indian life, like the tension between the rural and urban cultures, the joint family system, the individual's plight in the machine age, and the East-West encounter.

The earliest experiments in Indian English fiction during the first decade of the twentieth century show the writer's self-conscious use of the language. The kind of ornate Victorian English employed by the nationalistic writers in their non-fictional prose can be seen in the works of the pioneers in Indian English fiction too. Thus Kandan and Ramu, the characters in Venkataramani's fiction, speak in ornate and unnatural English. Perhaps it was only in the 1930s that the English sentence became shorter and the creative writers realized that English was no longer an alien tongue and that it could be bent to the shape they liked.

Like the non-fictional prose writer, the Indian English novelist too faces certain problems peculiar to his cultural situation. The language which he uses is not his first language. It is not the first language of the people about whom it is written. Moreover, for the English-speaking reader, the cultural factors that shape the Indian English fiction are entirely unknown. Consequently the writer faces the problem of rendering the nuances of the English language while conveying an essentially native sensibility. While handling a foreign medium, he has to explain certain subtleties in detail rather than take things for granted as it happens in fiction written in native languages.

Mulk Raj Anand employs the device of literal translation of Hindi or Punjabi idiom into English: *e.g.*, "May I be your sacrifice," or "Is this any talk?". Certain proverbs are translated into English: "After eating seven mice the cat is going on a pilgrimage." In the words of the rustic women in Raja Rao's fiction, the cat has "taken to asceticism only to commit more sins." Raja Rao coins new compound words like "Corner-House Moorthy," "*that-house* people," etc. Certain words of address like "Baba," "Dada," "Huzur," and "Malik" are freely used, as in Bhabani Bhattacharya's *He Who Rides a Tiger* or Manohar Malgaonkar's *The Princes.* The reader can find any number of usages like these in the course of his perusal of Indian English fiction.

NOTES

1. See N. Venkata Rao, "Pioneers of English Writing in India," *Annals of Oriental Research of the University of Madras,* XVIII, Part II, 1963.
2. J.J. Gumperz, "Hindi-Pubjabi Code-Switching in Delhi," *Proceedings of the Ninth International Congress of Linguistics* (Mouton, 1964) 116-17.
3. M.A.K. Halliday, *The Linguistic Sciences and Language Teaching* (Longmans, 1964) 294.
4. Shivendra K. Verma, "Swadeshi English: Form and Fiction" 6. (Paper presented at the Tenth International Congress of Ethnological and Anthropological Sciences, held in New Delhi, December 10-12, 1978.)
5. *Ibid.,* 4.
6. R.K. Narayan, *Reluctant Guru* (Delhi, 1974) 57.
7. "A Plea for English for Higher Education," *Language and Society in India: Transactions of Indian Institute of Advanced Study* (Simla, 1968), Vol. 8, 280.
8. "'Pigeon-Indian': Some Notes on Indian-English Writing," *Seminar on Australian and Indian Literature,* New Delhi, January 12-16, 1970: 8.

7

Mulk Raj Anand on the Novel*

Among the contemporary Indian English novelists, Mulk Raj Anand is one of the few writers having, what he would like to call, "certain hunches about the novel."[1] Even though he has not enunciated an elaborate theory of the novel, it is possible to see in his numerous letters, essays, and lectures the gradual evolution of an idea of the novel. The novel form to Anand has been a vehicle for conveying his deepest concern for the human predicament in the contemporary India. And one can see in his fictional idea an indisputable relationship between form and content.

In his remonstrance to Saros Cowasjee, Anand is not apparently in favour of the rigid stance of the formalists in fiction-writing. He says, adopting Roy Campbell's phrase, "What is the use of keeping the form, the kerb and the edge all right and destroy the bloody horse?"[2] In his review of Henry Green's *Loving*, he sets the perspective on form-content relationship:

> "...if I may venture an arbitrary dictum, I should say that the primary condition of art is not form but sensibility."[3]
>
> Furthermore,
>
> ...it is not enough to want to say something. Everything depends on how one says—how the imagination of a writer can transform the various realities, inter-penetrate characters with insight, and 'connect' the poetry and the prose.[4]

It is in such an "inter-penetration" of characters and in the "connecting" of the poetry and the prose that form becomes

* *Kakatiya Journal of English Studies* (Mulk Raj Anand Special Issue) I, i (Spring 1977), 190-99.

indispensable for an adequate expression of the artistic sensibility. Form and sensibility cannot be mutually exclusive. The writer's sensibility and his mode of expression shape each other. According to Northrop Frye,

> The word form has normally two complementary terms, matter and content, and it perhaps makes some distinction whether we think of form as a shaping principle or as a containing one. As shaping principle, it may be thought of as narrative, organizing temporally what Milton called, in an age of more exact terminology, the 'matter' of his song. As containing principle it may be thought of as meaning holding the poem together in a simultaneous structure.[5]

Form implies "meaning" which expresses the writer's "sensibility." The "shaping principle" and the "containing principle" together make up the work of literary art.

Anand's own "sensibility" finds expression through the specific forms of writing that he adopts in his work. A significant aspect of the form in his fictional composition is the stream of consciousness technique, even though he cannot entirely be identified with the Joycean school. Of course, Anand's connections with the Bloomsbury school are well-known. In his "Introduction" to the unpublished manuscript on *The Novel Form in the Ocean of Story*, he says:

> In Bloomsbury, I discovered Proust's long novel, *Remembrance of Things Past* in the brilliant transcreations of Scott Moncruff which absorbed me for years with its reiterations of feelings, in integral musical rhythms.[6]

Anand's initial jaunts into the world of the Bloomsbury school are thus a result of his enthusiasm for the "reiterations of feelings" and "integral musical rhythms." Krishan in *The Morning Face* declares:

> ...let me dedicate myself to that disordered imagination of the new poetry, beyond insipid harmonious rhymes, or passions sung and understood by the singer, away from pastimes, full of pain and ineffable torture and the utterest joy, not only in hexameters, but in the rich flow of words, like a river....[7]

By means of a "rich flow of words, like a river," Anand seems to make his character utter the poetic truth—the truth about the spectrum of life. Referring to *The Road*, Anand says in a letter to Saros Cowasjee:

> I, therefore, pursued the mirror game, at various levels of consciousness of the people, concave and convex, in this drama of the soul. You will notice that, technically, it is not a straight narrative, but diversified by breaking through the obvious planes to the impalpable world of feelings of the characters involved.[8]

Anand is concerned with telling the truth about his characters and in that truth he finds the poetry of human life. In order to give the fullest expression to this, he finds the stream of consciousness a convenient device. He uses the technique of the Joycean school to a limited extent in internalizing the character's experience. In probing into the mind of his characters, Anand aims to bring out what is essentially human in them, fusing the inner psychological reality with the outer social reality. The internal rhythm that he tries to establish in his characters should be in unison with the very rhythm of the life around. This, in fact, is the real poetry of Anand's fiction.

In spite of all his concern for the social condition both in his theory and practice, Anand is basically a novelist of character. Character as shaped by environment and strength of will forms the core of his fictional writing. As Anand himself has said in a recent letter to me,

> The zigzag of evolution always sparks off stagnant societies, the quick of which sets off various transformation and metamorphosis, followed by conservation and again to the struggles against slavery of mind and body.
>
> Underneath these processes the renewal of the individual, through confrontation of reality, compels human beings to renew themselves. But evolution has to be conscious of itself if we are not vegetables. And consciousness becomes the highest ideal of the awakening individual. The renewal is not an obvious or pre-determined Karmic process. It is a kind of evolutionary dialectic of conflicts, oppositions and labyrinthine rhythmic interplay and may

> possibly result in synthesis, through experience of life at various levels, in different situations.[9]

The individual, in Anand's view, is in the process of evolution and the purpose of the novelist is to depict such an evolution. Thus if it is not a "pre-determined Karmic process," it is "a kind of evolutionary dialectic of conflicts" that shapes character. However, Anand gives great significance to the "experience of life at various levels, in different situations." The "confrontation of reality" shapes the individual, and the purpose of the novelist, in Anand's view, is to depict such a reality. Another novelist who has said much about life and reality in fiction is Henry James. In this connection it may be profitable to compare the views of Anand and James. In his famous essay, "The Art of Fiction" (1884), James says that "A novel is a living thing, and all one and continuous, like any other organism, and in proportion as it lives will it be found, I think, that in each of the parts there is something of each of the other parts."[10] Also he exhorts the young novelist to "try and catch the color of life itself."[11] Mulk Raj Anand, in a lecture on the Indian English Novel, refers to "the flavour of life in our novels"[12] and says that

> ...the novelist is a new kind of god, who loves people, who overcomes his own isolation, puts his own knots alongside theirs, grows with them, manifests himself in the multiplicity of their beings and releases them into their own unique life, and co-exists with them in the joys and sorrows of their very human life.
>
> The novel, is, for me, the creative weapon for attaining humanness—it is the weapon of humanism.[13]

Thus, in Anand's view, the novelist is simultaneously close to the character and sufficiently detached to present him in his true colours. This omniscient narrator device enables the writer to probe into the very intricacies of the character.

To my query whether his own attitude to life or "the flavour of life" is similar to James's "color of life,[11] Anand replies:

> ...the novelist is constrained not merely to be a dispassionate observer of the fates but to be a philosopher committed to life against death. He has to make a total

> confrontation of our century, and to see every situation in this tragic period, from the point of view of how the urges of his characters for political freedom, and the other implied freedoms, can be expressed within the context of the art form of the novel.
>
> Of course, he must catch the 'color of life' itself, or its vitality, in all its ebb and flow. But when the 'unknown fate,' which is the new god of money and power hangs over the heads of all the characters, in all parts of the world, the clouds of war become denser, and the threat of the extinction of our planet looms large, the sombre atmosphere is bound to induce a melancholy in the soul: the colours of life are almost dimmed into the ashen grey of death.[14]

While both James and Anand stress the importance of the depiction of "life" in the novel, James is more a "dispassionate observer" of the fates of his characters whereas Anand seems to be deeply involved with "the unknown fate which is the new god of money and power" that "hangs over the heads of all the characters." The deeper emotional involvement of Anand in the life of his characters—the downtrodden—is evident when he says that "the colours of life are almost dimmed into the ashen grey of death."

Anand maintains that the writer voices the aspirations of the people:

> ...what is a writer if he is not the fiery voice of the people, who, through his own torments, urges and exaltations, by realizing the pains, frustrations and aspirations of others, and by cultivating his incipient powers of expression, transmutes in art all feeling, all thought, all experience—thus becoming the seer of a new vision in any given situation.[15]

This conception of the writer as a "seer of a new vision" reinforces Anand's idea of the novelist as a poet speaking to his own generation as well as to the future generations. His idea of the writer as a "fiery voice of the people" brings to one's mind E.M. Forster's definition of "Prophecy" as "a tone of voice."[16] Fiction, according to Forster, "always reaches back to pity and love. It is spasmodically realistic. And it gives us the sensation of a song or of sound."[17] Just as in Forster (writing about the Anglo-Indian world) there is an urge to convey a message to mankind, so also in Anand there is a "fiery voice" trying to make itself heard across the sub-continent. By means of "pity and love" for humanity, both the novelists visualize a glorious future for the world at large.

While describing the origin and development of the Indian novel, Anand expounds at length on "The Yoke of Pity" and says:

> This concept of Karuna or compassion came to men and women in travail as the first enunciation of expiation through art, centuries before Aristotle's famous *Katharsis.*[18]

"Catharsis," as it is employed by Aristotle in *The Poetics* in relation to tragedy, means the purging of the reader's or the spectator's emotions by evoking pity and terror at the suffering of the tragic hero. Anand's concept of Karuna or compassion implies "expiation through art." His tragic hero, the down-trodden, does not suffer from a tragic flaw in the Aristotelian sense of the term. On the other hand, the Bakhas of Anand's fictional world are victims of society, their fates having been determined by heredity and environment. But they struggle heroically to change the dispensation and suffer in the process.

Compassion, as Anand defines it, is similar to what Elizabeth K. Adams, in her book, *The Aesthetic Experience* calls "aesthetic sympathy." Such a sympathy is always at the heart of a social determination of reality. In that sympathy, the opposition between individual and society breaks down.[19] As Adams suggests in a quotation from Tolstoy's *What is Art*?'

> A real work of art destroys in the consciousness of the receiver the separation between himself and the artist... In this freeing of our personality from its separation and isolation, in this uniting it with others, lies the chief characteristic of the great attractive force of art.[20]

The basic connection between the social determination of reality and the aesthetic enjoyment of a work of art seems to be in Anand's mind when he asserts:

> ...my aim is not negative, merely to shock, but to stimulate consciousness at all levels.[21]

If Anand's idea concerning the aim of a work of art is somewhat different from Aristotle's "Catharsis," it is nevertheless aesthetic in its connotation in that it aims "to stimulate consciousness." Anand aims to arouse the reader to the consciousness of life's basic problems in the contemporary situation. In this sense he is no doubt a superb literary artist, actively writing fiction and theorizing about fiction.

NOTES

1. Letter to me dated December 17, 1976.
2. Letter to Saros Cowasjee dated October 25, 1970. Quoted in Saros Cowasjee, "Anand's Literary Creed," *The Journal of Indian Writing in English* No. 1 (January, 1973) 66.
3. Review of Henry Green's *Loving in Life and Letters To-day,* Vol. 46, No. 95 (July, 1945) 55.
4. Mulk Raj Anand, "Creative Writing in Present Crisis," *Indian Literature,* VI, No. l, 1963: 74.
5. Northrop Frye, *Anatomy of Criticism: Four Essays* (Princeton: Princeton University Press, 1957) 83.
6. "Introduction" to Anand's unpublished Ms. on *The Novel Form in the Ocean of Story.* He also says, "James Joyce's banned book *Ulysses* was, however, the rage in Western Europe during the early twenties when I reached London. And naturally, I tried to absorb his daring experiments in word-coinage, fragmentation of language and rhythmic flow, by tracing his development from *A Portrait of the Artist as a Young Man* to Work in Progress, later to be called *Finnegan's Wake.*"
7. Mulk Raj Anand, *The Morning Face* (1968; rpt. New Delhi: Arnold-Heinemann, 1976) 571.
8. Saros Cowasjee, *Author to Critic: The Letters of Mulk Raj Anand* (Calcutta: Writers Workshop, 1973) 124.
9. Letter to me dated December 17, 1976.
10. *Henry James: Representative Selections,* ed. Lyon N. Richardson (New York: American Book Company, 1941) 86.
11. *Ibid.,* 97.
12. Mulk Raj Anand, *Roots and Flowers* (Dharwar: Karnatak University Press, 1972) 36.
13. *Ibid.*
14. Letter to me dated January 21, 1977.
15. "Pigeon-English: Some Notes on Indian English Writing," Anand's

lecture in a Seminar on Australian and Indian literature delivered in January 1970.

16. E.M. Forster, *Aspects of the Novel* (1927; rpt. Harmondsworth: Penguin Books Ltd., 1962) 129.
17. *Ibid.*, 140.
18. Chapter on "The Yoke of Pity" in the unpublished Ms. on *A Novel Form in the Ocean of the Story.*
19. Quoted in Max I. Baym, *A History of Literary Aesthetics in America* (New York: Frederick Unger Publishing Co., 1973) 146.
20. *Ibid.*
21. Saros Cowasjee, *Author to Critics: The Letters of Mulk Raj Anand* (Calcutta: Writers Workshop, 1973) 115-16.

8

ANAND'S VISION OF WAR AND DEATH IN *ACROSS THE BLACK WATERS**

Despite the tendency of scholars to treat Mulk Raj Anand as a writer concerned only with the rustics and the down-trodden, there are several other facets of his genius like art and cross-cultural studies. Coming after *Untouchable* (1933), *Across the Black Waters* (1940) deals with the larger human concerns of war and death in the context of the protagonist's encounter with the western culture. Read in the light of modern war literature, Anand's fictional rendering of World War I is amazingly refreshing, in spite of the rusticity of the characters involved.

As the second of the Lalu trilogy, *Across the Black Waters* follows *The Village* (1939) which ends with Lalu's joining the Indian sepoys bound for Vilayat (England). As Anand tells us before the opening of the novel, he wrote the first draft of *Across the Black Waters* in Barcelona, Madrid during January and April 1937 and rewrote it at Chinnoor, Oxfordshire between July and December 1939. The novel was based on the author's impressions of the Spanish Civil War as well as his own imagination or recollections of those who fought in Flanders. In a recent interview to *The New Indian Express,* Anand says: "I spent several months at Flanders to get the feel of the situation and only then did I embark on writing the book."[1] As many as 1200 of the British Indian army went to Flanders and only 50 of them came back after the War was over. Hence he says, "I wanted to bring out the pathos."[2] Translated into eleven European languages, the novel has recently been

* LITTCRIT, Vol. 26, Nos. 1 & 2, June-December 2000, 70-78.

adapted by the British Council into a play to mark the 80th anniversary of the end of World War I. The play travelled all over England and a seminar on the novel was held in Birmingham.

Whereas in *Untouchable* and other novels dealing with the social theme, Anand is concerned with suffering inflicted on the downtrodden, in *Across the Black Waters,* he deals with the humanistic theme in respect to the ruthless destruction of man by man with the machine. The pity of it is the soldiers, whether rustic or otherwise, are generally those joining the army to win bread for their families.

Referring to Lal Singh, K.R. Srinivasa Iyengar says: "His heart beats in response to the primordial life of the village, but his mind incessantly rebels and yearns for the dim, distant, alluring horizons."[3] In fact, it is not for any such idealistic concerns that Lal Singh goes out of his village Nandpur but as an escape from the vicious climate around, as an act of desperation. This, of course, is a blessing in disguise for him since the full potential in him emerges and he could achieve self-realization in his encounters abroad. Towards the end of *Across the Black Waters,* Lalu reflects on fate, reminiscing his life in Nandpur culminating in his narrow escape: "And then the landlord and the police had come up with a warrant for his arrest on a trumped up charge and he ran away.... The only escape from prison was to join the army."[4] The self-realization or growth of the adolescent hero is, in fact, his struggle for survival. Lal Singh's defiant nature is evident from the fact that he as a Sikh cuts his hair and registers as a Dogra. While he was helpless back home, he has his ultimate revenge on the foreign soil, as fate would have it. This is what Anand calls "Kismet" (299). Lalu has to play out his destined role and grow into full manhood, defying even death. It is not the situation of a mercenary for money alone to pay off debts to the landlord. It is destiny that elevates to heroism the otherwise nondescript individual, bringing him laurels; and his adversaries stand exposed in all their small-mindedness. As Alastair Niven says, "Anand's overriding concern in *Across the Black Waters,* almost the sole preoccupation of the novel, is with the devastating effect of war upon the individual."[5] Anand's clear message on the individual level in respect to the protagonist is that the course of destiny cannot be changed by the mighty. While the powerful landlord and the police stand reduced to insignificance, Lal Singh emerges as a war hero abroad. Even on the front, of course, he has to face petty jealousies and prejudices like those of Subah who tries to get Lalu courtmartialed but makes a fool of himself due to the sagacity of Ajitan Sahib.

Lalu and the other sepoys, even though bound ostensibly for Vilayat (England), find their ship docking in French waters. For Lalu, surviving the voyage across the ocean with its deep blue ("black") waters is a matter for thanksgiving to the Heavens:

> So we have come across the black waters safely, he said to himself apprehensively, as if he really expected some calamity, the legendary fate of all those who went beyond the seas, to befall him at any moment. Truly, the black, or rather blue, water seemed uncanny, spreading for thousands of miles (8).

To the superstitious rustics, the "blackness" of the sea waters is associated with death because the voyage is into the realm of the Unknown.

In "Eagles and Pigeons," Mustafa survives the shipwreck confronting a situation Lalu refers to as the "legendary fate of all those who went beyond the seas." As Mustafa says,

> I always laughed at the Mullah for saying everything was ordained by God, and mocked at my mother for believing in Fate, and I still don't believe in either, but I tell you one thing—the moment when Life meets Death is frightening.[6]

It is this point of Life meeting Death that causes the grimness of the novel *Across the Black Waters.* In the midst of the combat, with the rising tension among the soldiers and heart-burn caused by the conflict with the officers, "They had no hope or faith in their hearts except the fate to which they had resigned themselves, their Kismet, which, more and more, had begun to look like the premonition of a horrible death" (251). The soldiers experience comeraderie in the face of a common doom going to befall soon. In the midst of the gun fire, the sepoys seem to be engaged in a quest, sitting "patient and tranquil though rather pale and silent, as if they were reflecting on their docm...each to his own, as if everyone were alone in this ordeal" (142). As J. Glenn Gray says in *The Warriors,*

> ...the soldier who has yielded himself to the fortunes of war, has sought to kill and to escape, being killed, or who has even lived long enough in the disordered landscape of battle, is no longer what he was.... His moods and disposition are affected by the presence of others and the encompassing environment of threat and fear....[7]

Lalu and companions on the front are involved in such a situation. They are faced with the mounting fear caused by the "army machine" which works "with the ponderous efficiency of a force which had, for the time being, ground out all individual considerations" (233). Anand's vision of war reminds us of what Simone Weill says:

> As soon as the practice of war has revealed the fact that each moment holds the possibility of death, the mind becomes incapable of moving from one day to the next day without passing through the spectre of death....[8]

In dealing with the plight of the Indian sepoys in Flanders in 1914, Anand seems to be making a universal statement concerning the nature of war. His description of the appalling brutalities of war on account of his deep compassion for human suffering reminds us of the rendition of the effects of war by poets like Wilfred Owen, Siegfried Sassoon, and David Jones. Like the English poets, Anand too successfully evokes the pity of war and the poetry that is in the pity.

As the regiment of the Indian sepoys starts marching towards the battle front, the novelist reflects on the insanity of war:

> The element of sanity in Lalu persisted in the face of guns and in the face of the insanity which had blown off the towers of the churches, and he could not believe that ordinary men and women of good sense, and the Governments of France, England and Germany, which were saner and wiser than the ordinary people over whom they ruled, could be engaged in a war in which men were being killed and wounded and houses shattered (92-93).

Kirpu feels that even the rats in the sahibs' houses seem shrewd and wonders why such rich people "are killing each other and making a large graveyard of this land" (197). Bishop Padre, who visits the soldiers in the midst of the war, says it is "a holy war" (309). When Lalu observes the bonhomie among the enemies, the British and German soldiers, on Christmas day, he wonders at the "mockery of war" (303).

Across the Black Waters has a cultural dimension presented through interaction among the Indian sepoys and their general reaction to the British officers. Of course, heroism and the use of the machine on the front may cross all cultural barriers since the soldiers go desperate in the face of the death. Initially, on arrival at the French port and marching through the streets of Marseilles, the Indian soldiers with their rustic backgrounds experience culture shock. The scarcely clad French girls, the public hugging and kissing of men and women, the dancing couples and the "pleasures of Vilayat" are the initial surprises to the Indian soldiers. Anand comments on the class difference between the British and Indian officers (38), the Angrezi and the Indians, the sahibs and sepoys. There are divisions among the sepoys too—the sneaks, the shirkers, and the twisters. There is greater discipline on the part of the British officers and warmer officer-soldier relationship. The Indian sepoys are generally loyal to the British: "We have eaten the salt," Daddy Dhanoo says, "It is a question of gratitude" (137). Despite the Indian soldiers' amazement at the glitter abroad, there is a sense of the superior on their part. Daddy Dhanoo says with derision, "They have no religion. No law. They drink wine and make eyes at women. They believe in this life only eat, drink, shit!" (73).

Lalu's own reaction to these things around him is one of "emptiness from the centre of which his two eyes seemed to see this world as an enormous enclosure, crowded by hordes of hard, gigantic shapes which were oppressing him" (56). This sense of loneliness has been in the very nature of the youth from his days at Nandpur. On looking at the statue of Joan of Arc, Lalu is reminded of Rani of Jhansi and feels "the blood coursing in his veins with the ambition to follow her on the path of glory" (41). In fact, Lalu as the centre of all conflict, is in the process of a movement from war within to war without. For him the confrontation now is not with social forces but elemental forces.

While in the trenches, "the boy" Lalu is "frightened like a baby" (188). Seeing bayonet attacks on the battlefield, he is reminded of the oxen butchered by the village cobbler. He trembles "like the school boy, the dread loomed before his eyes" (142). On seeing the train of wounded soldiers, Lalu swoons: "A sudden tremor of dread spread like a panic in his brain.... It seemed unending, this torturous journey into the Unknown" (78-79). He feels: "If one who slays one is a murderer then he who slays a thousand is not a hero" (137). Referring to modern terror caused by the World War, Frederick J. Hoffman says: "The word *murder* no longer has any meaning in a situation permitting a mass production of corpses."[9] Lalu suffers a conflict within himself:

> In him the two poles of nature seemed always to have been quarrelling, as if he had not decided whether to burst out of his skin, as it were, and live outside himself, or to recline back, self-exiled, pain-marred, mutilated with the memories of those hindrances which the world had put in his way. The two anti-types had revolved in a furious whirl of the axle tree during his boyhood. He was the contradiction who had cultivated a pride in excess of a dignity, even as he had gone carelessly about, playing pranks with the boys of his village and laughing at the grey beards, bent on the consummation of his unrestricted impulses, as if he could cheat nature and take happiness by surprise (277).

The deaths of Daddy Dhanoo, Lakhman Singh and Uncle Kirpu intensely agitate Lalu and with his "ego looming larger and larger," he says, "So, after all I am in for it" (280).

Alastair Niven says that Lalu and the sepoys are rustics, unsuited to modern warfare, are "herded by the thousand to fight in Europe for the King Emperor."[10] The Indian soldiers do fight despite their rusticity once they are on the front. Whatever the cultural background of the soldier, he has no identity. As Frederick J. Hoffman rightly observes, the soldier is "unknown," existing in "a state of unreality, anonymity."[11] In this connection, it is interesting to compare Anand's *Across the Black Waters* with Stephen Crane's *The Red Badge of Courage*

(1895). Henry Fleming, the protagonist in Crane's novel, is generally called "the youth," or "he," and he is an inexperienced soldier, "an unknown quantity," torn between a "little panic-fear" and "visions of broken-bladed glory" as he faces his first battle in the Civil War. Determined to be a hero, Fleming suddenly turns coward. He then recovers and behaves as the fighter he had wished to be. In both the novels the theme is that man's salvation lies in change and spiritual growth. It is only by immersion in the flux of experience that man becomes disciplined or develops in character, conscience or soul. Whatever the intensity of fear presented in the novels in the face of combat, it is the self-combat of the youth who fears and initially resists change and spiritual growth. Fleming fearlessly plunges into battle, charging the enemy like "a pagan who defends his religion."[12]

As a typical War novel, *Across the Black Waters* has in its texture the theme of not only death but also of love. One of the greatest American War novels, Ernest Hemingway's *For Whom the Bell Tolls* (1940) depicts the hero Robert Jordan's love for Maria in the midst of war. Having planned a trilogy, Anand was obviously anxious to bring his hero Lal Singh back to India for the third novel, *The Sword and the Sickle* (1942). If he allowed Lalu to die on the battlefield as his final noble act of sacrifice in the context of the deaths of his dear friends, Anand's novel would have achieved the poignancy of Hemingway's novel, which resulted from the American author's journalistic adventures in the Spanish Civil War. Some of the deeper strengths of Hemingway's novel come from his long involvement with Spain, as Carlos Baker tells us.[13] Interestingly, Anand's War novel too was based upon his personal experiences in Spain. Robert Jordan's story acquires its poignancy from the fact that he is guided by the conviction that man's chief duty is to do everything he can do for collective human dignity and freedom and that it is the individual's chief obligation to sacrifice himself for the human community which is his greatest opportunity for a transcendent act. As Jordan says, fatally wounded and lying on the hillside almost delirious, "I have fought for what I believed in for a year now. If we win here we will win everywhere. The world is a fine place and worth the fighting for...."[14] Jordan has the choice between love and duty before the bridge-blowing. The bliss of his love for Maria is the great compensation for the inevitability of catastrophe. However, his sense of duty obliterates anything else. In Anand's novel *Across the Black Waters* too love is the only refuge in the midst of the unmitigated horrors of war and forebodings of death. Lalu, having been "the dehumanized toy of destiny," and "in the face of the unknown, in full view of the spectacle of destruction and death," yields to the "strange purblind tenderness of love" (239). As uncle Kirpu says, "love is to escape from this beastliness" of war (241-43). Ever since Lalu sees Marie, as he and the other sepoys are playing on the bank of the stream, he has been fascinated by her looks, and "she seemed to have wrought some magic on Lalu" (224). The innocence and beauty of the girl, in contrast to the ferocity of the war, greatly fascinate him, "his head surcharged with madness" (225). On account of his love for Marie, Lalu has to face the jealousy of Subah Singh who tries to get Lalu court-martialed. Notwithstanding these things, Lalu has to march forward on the battlefield: "Abjectly grateful for the smaller mercies of life, he sought to crush the luxury of desire and went about like the dehumanized toy of destiny, which was the unknown will of the Sarkar" (239). Henceforward he plunges into the battle, prepared for annihilation as per the will of the Unknown Sarkar above, the ultimate destiny that governs human life: "Lalu felt intoxicated by the urge to get to the crest and ran forward blindly" (321). Wounded by a bullet that has pierced through the calf of his leg, he falls, face forward. By the time he opens his eyes, he finds himself being dragged by a German soldier, and "He resigned himself to the mercy of his captors" (322).

Anand has successfully evoked the atmosphere of war in which the Indian sepoys fight alongside the British in a magnificent display of bravery and loyalty. The masterful depiction of the combat on the front in *Across the Black Waters* equals the skills of writers of War novels like Stephen Crane and Ernest Hemingway. The unknown rustic Indian soldier displays the courage and conviction equal to that of any Western war hero. It is at these levels that Anand achieves universalization of presenting the horrors of war as well as the pity that it evokes.

NOTES

1. Vinita Deshmukh, "Going Global from Khandala," *The New Indian Express,* January 24, 1999.
2. *Ibid.*
3. K.R. Srinivasa Iyengar, *Indian Writing in English* (New Delhi: Sterling Publishers Pvt. Ltd., 1962) 347.
4. Mulk Raj Anand, *Across the Black Waters* (1949; Delhi: Orient Paperbacks, 1980) 301. Hereafter page references to this edition are given in parentheses.
5. Alastair Niven, *The Yoke of Pity: A Study in the Fictional Writings of Mulk Raj Anand* (New Delhi: Arnold-Heinemann, 1978) 71.
6. Mulk Raj Anand, "Eagles and Pigeons," *The Barber's Trade Union and Other Stories* (London: Jonathan Cape, 1944) 171.
7. J. Glenn Gray, *The Warriors* (New York: Harcourt, Brace, 1959) 27.
8. Simon Weill, "The 'Iliad' Poem of Might," *Intimations of Christianity,* tr. Elizabeth C. Geissbuhler (Boston: Beacon Press, 1958) 41.
9. Frederick J. Hoffman, *The Mortal No: Death and the Modern Imagination* (Princeton: Princeton University Press, 1964) 269.
10. Alastair Niven 68.
11. Frederick J. Hoffman 15.
12. Stephen Crane, *The Red Badge of Courage* (1894; New York: The Modern Library, 1951) 194-95.
13. Carlos Baker, *Ernest Hemingway: A Life Story* (New York: Scribner's, 1969) 302-30; 345-48.
14. Ernest Hemingway, *For Whom the Bell Tolls* (New York: Scribner's, 1940) 502.

9

BHABANI BHATTACHARYA'S *A DREAM IN HAWAII*: A STUDY IN POSTCOLONIAL SPIRITUALITY*

Postcolonial writing attempts relocation of the self and retrieval of the native culture from foreign dominance. Whether it is a travelogue of a Western writer of Indian origin or Indian writer aiming to reach out to the Western readership, there is an interaction between the Eastern and Western sensibilities. The degree of cultural amalgamation or conflict depends upon the maturity of the sensibility of the writer. Gayatri Chakravorty Spivak refers to "the specific intellectual" and "the universal intellectual."[1] The question is whether the intellectual—writer of a travelogue, novelist, or philosopher—can rise above the limited sphere of his own specific culture and attain the universal level. The postcolonial Indian English writers of fiction have been engaged in this intellectual exploration depicting both the specific Indian culture and the hybridization of Indian culture on account of the Western impact. These cultural cross-currents have been vibrant in the post-Independence times, the writers giving literary expression to cultural displacement and discontinuity. As Jahan Ramazani says, "Postcolonialism is concerned with what has been called 'the location of culture.'"[2] The "location" may not sometimes be specifically geographical on account of universal values. Cultural reversal and displacement may result in what Spivak calls "the binary opposition, the Western intellectual's longing for all that is not West, ...the so-called non-West's turn toward the West."[3] It will be interesting to see this displacement or transfer of literary sensibility in the writings of Indian writers

---

* *Kakatiya Journal of English Studies*, Vol. 18/1993, 45-52.

of fiction in English with special reference to Bhabani Bhattacharya's *A Dream in Hawaii* (1978).

I

Ever since Indians began writing in English, the East-West Encounter has been a major theme engaging their attention. After India's independence from British rule, the influence of the British and Western institutions and habits continues to be prevalent.

The postcolonial experience dealing with the political and social issues has been rendered exquisitely by major novelists like Mulk Raj Anand, R.K. Narayan, Anita Desai, Kamala Markandaya, Nayantara Sahgal, and Bhabani Bhattacharya. Kamala Markandaya looks at the Swami cult affecting the modern Indian society in *A Silence of Desire* (1961) and *Possession* (1963) from a perspective more mundane than Raja Rao's in *The Serpent and the Rope* (1960). R.K. Narayan's *The Guide* (1959) depicts Raju, after his love affair with Rosie and the prison term, initially masquerading as a Swami and finally achieving self-realization.

Bhabani Bhattacharya in *He Who Rides a Tiger* (1955) describes the social and religious hypocrisy resulting from the Bengal famine in the post-Independence India. Due to hunger and ill-treatment, Kalo avenges on society by transforming himself into Mangal Adhikari, the brahmin and performs a "miracle": a Shiva *linga* emerging from the ground. By means of this feat, he plays upon the popular credulity to miracles and reaps dividends. His daughter, Lekha, also a victim of society, becomes the Mother of the Sevenfold Bliss and the object of adoration. Bhattacharya attacks the superstitions and rituals corrupting the Hindu society. Kalo says: "While men died of hunger, wealth grew and while kindliness dried up religion was more in demand."[4] It is only the veneer of religion since the same people would not bother to look at destitutes dying. The novelist exposes falsehood in religion through the words of Biten: "Food for the soul is produced and sold like food for stomach, and though the ways of the two trades are different, you pay for both with hard cash. The temple is a market and the priest a dealer. People are always ready to pay well for feeding the inner man" (43). The novelist describes people's belief in the Yogis and Mothers. Lekha takes recourse to rituals for solace to overcome the grief caused by Biten. Referring to Lekha's touching the forehead of a sick child with her toe and the death of the child, Orvelle Prescott says: "Mr Bhattacharya deplores the suffering caused by blind acceptance of the caste system, and yet pities the blind believer."[5] Whether it is the caste system or hunger or superstition, Bhattacharya exposes the binary attitude concerning religion in the postcolonial India.

In Raja Rao's *The Serpent and the Rope* (1960), the real problem for the central character Rama, consequent upon his sensual involvement with Madeleine and Savitri, is to attain inner harmony. Man, entangled in the web of *maya,* takes as serpent what is after all a rope. As Rama tells Madeleine, "The Guru brings you the lantern; the road is seen, the long, white road, going with the statutory stars."[6] The search for the Guru and inner harmony, rendered by Raja Rao in highly complex Vedantic and aesthetic terms, can also be seen in the real life experience of the Westerners and the Westernized Indians in the postcolonial times.

Contemporary man, caught in the whirlpool of the dehumanizing life, looks desperately for succour, seeking peace either in drugs or in the proliferating cults. Taking advantage of this situation, self-seeking Mammon-worshippers—Gurus, Maharishis, and Yogis—have launched spiritual movements and established posh "ashrams" to preach instant meditation. As a result of these perversions and ungodly activities, the very meaning of meditation—*dhyana*—as enunciated in the great Hindu scriptures like the Vedas and *Bhagavad Gita*—is lost on the contemporary man. The concept of Guru, enunciated in the Holy Books, has taken on such perverted meanings in the popular understanding that Peter Brent says:

> For Indians, particularly those of the middle classes, there are only two directions they can go to prove that they can love, and be loved. One is towards homosexuality, the other towards the Guru—the two not being mutually exclusive.[7]

Referring to the "Swami" in Indian English fiction, K.R. Srinivasa Iyengar says: "Sometimes the Swamy or Sadhu has no more than a decorative role; he is there because Western readers look for him in novels on India."[8] However, whether it is treated seriously by Raja Rao or in sarcastic terms by Bhabani Bhattacharya, the Swamy motif in Indian English fiction constitutes the binary opposition in the postcolonial Indian English fiction—between materialism and spirituality.

II

In Bhabani Bhattacharya's *A Dream in Hawaii* (1978), as in Raja Rao's *The Serpent and the Rope* (1960), the quest is that of an academic for spirituality despite his sensual involvements. The binary opposition of the sensual and the spiritual determines character and action. Instead of leaving the reader lost in the web of Advaita philosophy, Bhattacharya brings him closer to the contemporary predicament. Swami Yogananda, following his erotic adventures with his student Devjani at an Indian university, gives up his professorship and dons saffron robes. At the invitation of the East-West Center, he goes to Hawaii to give a course of lectures on Eastern Philosophy—"to present Universal Religion in its Vedantic concept."[9] He is engaged in a relentless quest for "reality behind the appearances which were *maya,* the stuff of illusion." Several disturbed souls like Jennifer, the socialite and Stella the Ph.D. student in Hinduism, caught in "the crisis in a sick society," look up to him for spiritual help. There are others like Professor Walt Gregson, the estranged husband of Stella and Dr Vincent Swift, the culture-vulture, who question Yogananda's true credentials to spirituality. Yogananda has taught Philosophy for six years in the Indian universities before becoming "Swamy," and at thirty he is "one of India's famed spiritual leaders" (29). He would like to be different from others of his kind and hence he is clean-shaven unlike the bearded *sadhus.*

In spite of his discourses on *Bhagavadgita* to a captivated American audience and his attempts at *dhyana,* Yogananda is haunted by disturbing memories of his affair with Devjani at the Indian university and even in Hawaii he looks for her. He utterly fails to achieve the kind of detachment that is prescribed in Chapter VI ("The Yoga of Meditation") of

Bhagavadgita as being the essential requisite for prayer. The Lord says:

> So, with his heart serene and fearless,
> Firm in the vow of renunciation,
> Holding the mind from its restless roaming,
> Now let him struggle to reach my openness.[10]

Swami Yogananda, despite his saffron robes, has failed to hold his mind "from its restless roaming." In the words of the author of the novel, "The process of sublimation had its own rules, he would point to himself. His submerged mind could not be controlled, nature's compulsions could not be denied" (44). Even as a Swami Yogananda lay asleep, "he was in the act of making love. That act possessed him" (44).

Ironically, Yogananda's attempts at spiritual experience take place in the enchanting atmosphere of the beautiful island of Hawaii, a pleasure resort of the most materialistic kind. The sight of "the body's bareness" on the Waikiki beach makes him feel "enchanted." The result is spiritual disenchantment for him. The "reality" that he is searching for proves an illusion. The Guru that the disturbed Americans see in him is himself torn by doubt about his own spiritual integrity and he returns to India. While the effect of Swami Yogananda's experience on the reader is one of the comic, what is ultimately significant in Bhattacharya's presentation in *A Dream in Hawaii* is the Kiplingesque awareness that East is East and West is West.

Bhabani Bhattacharya brings out the binary opposition not only in the East-West encounter but also within the East and within the West separately. This multidimensional conflict determines the social and spiritual aspects of the postcolonial life. Transference, displacement, and alienation constitute the postcolonial experience of not only the Indians settled or born abroad, but also of the Indians in India due to the Western impact. The basic conflict in human nature is presented by Bhattacharya in *A Dream in Hawaii* involving movement between realms. The "movement" may be different from that of the Indians abroad, born or settled there. It is that of the natives like Yogananda experiencing alienation within their own culture due to the cross-currents of emotional and spiritual problems.

In *A Dream in Hawaii*, the shifting of scenes from India to America and in flashback from America to India is like displacement in the postcolonial sense. In India, when Yogananda comes from Rishikesh and lectures in Delhi, the unsophisticated crowd might have applauded him without understanding the profundities involved. But the applause from the American audience is of lost souls in search of a spiritual mirage.

When Swami Yogananda says, "Our Ancient Philosophy is boldly modern in its own way. The West has read that same story in our ancient temple sculptures at Konark, at Khajuraho!" (18), Stella feels, "Within him the East and the West so readily coalesced!" (18). Ironically, this coalescence goes counter to Yogananda's preaching of *dhyana* which leaves him confused. It is not the external East-West conflict but the inner turmoil of his own soul that disturbs Yogananda. This is the basic binary opposition.

Another level of binary opposition is in Stella with her vain spiritual yearnings as Yogananda's disciple and her conflict with her materialistic husband, Walt. While Stella is looking for solace in philosophy, Walt is seeking "correlations of life and literature as part of his study" (21). Walt tells Stella that he would like to "ask the Swami one or two questions in the context of what he calls crisis in a sick society: that is, our American society" (24). As Walt asserts, "The crises we know are beyond his limited range of experience" (27). The disturbances deep within the soul of Yogananda are evident. Stella recalls that as soon as Swami Yogananda is received at the airport, by members of the Indian Association, he inquired about Devjani. In the flashback is given an account of Yogananda's lecture on Eastern Philosophy at the Indian university where Devjani was a student:

> The instructor has an unseemly impulse: To undo the braided hair and let the dishevelled mass cascade over her bosom!... An odd wish for a man trying to explain Vedantic monism! (13)

At the Kennedy Theatre of the University of Hawaii, following the applause at Swami Yogananda's lecture, Stella reflects: "The Swami's relentless quest was directed to the core of reality behind the appearances which were *maya*, the stuff of illusion" (8). The suggestion is which is reality and which the illusion in Swami Yogananda himself.

Dr Vincent Swift is introduced to Swami Yogananda by Stella as "our topmost exponent of cultureways" (52). Hawaii is the "unique East-West mix. The strong inter-culturation" (56). When confronted by Dr. Swift to comment on the celibacy of the Indian yogis, Swami Yogananda is bewildered. As Swift says to Yogananda, "One expects from an alien analyst of our sick ways something more than hackneyed repetitions" (60). Dr. Swift ridicules Yogananda's visit to America to re-enact the visit of Swami Vivekananda:

> Now, could it be that Swami Yogananda's mystical experience which made him reborn is relevant to a certain memorable day in the Vivekananda story? A day that is exactly a hundred years old? (62)

Yogananda has come to America to represent Universal Religion in its Vedantic concept. Dr Swift would like to set up an institute offering practical help to reduce inner tensions—such help drawn best from Indian know-how and wisdom. Dr. Swift would expect Yogananda himself shed a little of the ancient India in him and absorb a little of Modern America. He feels that is the only way to harmonize diverse cultures: "World culture could have no reality unless based on the broadest spectrum of interchange" (144). Such mutually opposed views concerning cultural interaction causes insurmountable obstacles. The binary opposition makes the lofty ideal of "world culture" only a dream. This seems to be the ultimate message of Bhabani Bhattacharya in the novel.

Referring to the ecstasy of the dancers of the Hare Krishna Movement, Stella wonders:

> Our American society with its contradictions! Violence in its most brutal forms rages through the nation and tries to destroy every civilized norm. Yet a great search goes on widening, the search for...shall I say, a new world aching to be born? Two contrary ways running parallel. Where will victory be? (72)

In addition to the other binaries of characters and ideas in the novel, the basic contradiction within the American culture itself is paradoxical: the dualism of violence alongside an impassioned search, "a search rooted in depths of longing for the new world yet to be born" (73), as Stella says. The dualism is also the result of a paradoxical presence of Puritanism and permissiveness in the American society. Another paradox is in the super technology hitting at the very roots of traditionalism, resulting in counter-culture.

Whatever the vain attempts of an Indian Swami like Yogananda, himself torn between contradictions, to cure the "sick society," the binaries within himself and within the postcolonial Indian culture are pitted against the binaries of the American culture in particular and the Western culture in general. Consequently, the opposition remains.

NOTES

1. Gayatri Chakravorty Spivak, *The Post-Colonial Critic: Interviews, Strategies, Dialogues* (New York: Routledge, 1990) 3.
2. Jahan Ramazani, "Metaphor and Postcoloniality: The Poetry of A.K. Ramanujan," *Contemporary Literature*, Vol. 39, No. 1 (Spring 1998) 28.
3. Spivak 8.
4. Bhabani Bhattacharya, *He Who Rides a Tiger* (New Delhi: Hind Pocket Books, 1955) 113. Page references are given in parentheses after each quotation from the text.
5. Orvelle Prescott, "Books of the Times," *The New York Times*, December 28, 1954.
6. Raja Rao, *The Serpent and the Rope* (1960: rpt. New Delhi: Oxford University Press, 1978) 192.
7. Peter Brent, *Godmen of India* (Harmondsworth: Penguin, 1968) 16.
8. K.R. Srinivasa Iyengar, *Indian Writing in English* (New Delhi: Sterling Publishers Pvt. Ltd., 1984) 328.
9. Bhabani Bhattacharya, *A Dream in Hawaii* (New Delhi: Macmillan, 1978) 144. Page references are given in parentheses after each quotation from the text.
10. *The Song of God: Bhagavad Gita*. Trans. Swami Prabhavananda and Christopher Isherwood (New York: The New American Library Inc., 1951) 65.

10

PHILOSOPHERS AND LOVERS: PARADOX OF EXPERIENCE IN SHIV K. KUMAR'S *THE BONE'S PRAYER**

Indian English novelists like Mulk Raj Anand, Raja Rao, R.K. Narayan, Anita Desai, and Kamala Markandaya have dealt with the East-West question and the emotional involvement of men and women from a variety of perspectives. While Mulk Raj Anand and R.K. Narayan have considered these on the plane of external reality either seriously or in subtle comic vein, Raja Rao dives deeper into the inner reality describing the spiritual experiences of intellectuals following their emotional involvements. More recently, Bhabani Bhattacharya in *A Dream in Hawaii* (1978) and Shiv K. Kumar in *The Bone's Prayer* (1979) have pondered over these emotional and spiritual experiences of intellectual men and women in contemporary life, at the same time exposing much that is sham. In this sense their novels are somewhat different from Raja Rao's *The Serpent and the Rope* which depicts the central character Rama's quest for inner harmony following his sensual involvement with Madeleine and Savitri.

Despite its affinities with Raja Rao's *The Serpent and the Rope* and Bhattacharya's *A Dream in Hawaii,* Shiv K. Kumar's *The Bone's Prayer* is multi-dimensional in its meaning. One can see in it not only the conventional aspects of the Indian English novel like the East-West encounter, spiritual quest, and the Indian society, but the more universal elements like human sympathy, personal friendship, and tragic betrayal in

* CYGNUS (Lucknow), No. 1, 1979, 56-59.

love, depicted in a poetic atmosphere of evocative power and beauty. Rendered in a deceptively simple style, the novel is remarkable for the powerful irony of character and situation.

While the first part of the novel is in first-person narration by Sunil Sharma and is interesting for his self-revelation, ratiocination, and ironic comment on the social and religious humbug in modern life, the second part relates in epistolary technique the philosopher Suresh Gupta's experiences at Elmira that ultimately drive him to suicide. Suresh gets entangled in two successive love affairs—first with his freedom-loving student Sheila in Chandigarh and then in America with another student Caroline Gunther, the divorcee, who runs away with an American guitarist. It is only in his brief affairs with Mona, the Goanese call-girl, that he comes close to the bliss of human love "through a mutual realization of pain as the ultimate reality" (135).

The central focus of *The Bone's Prayer* is on this pain and suffering, culminating in death for the realization of unending bliss of love. In the process the characters undergo excruciating tension between involvement and withdrawal. Suresh Gupta experiences the initial bliss of love when he gets involved with his student Sheila, but her secret affair with his own cousin Bhoj brings him the first shock of his life. Thereafter, Sheila's "free love" and Suresh's yearning for the ideal love are at variance with each other. The ironic reference to the "Holy Grail"—Suresh's discovery of Sheila's brooch in the hotel room at Bikrata—reinforces the novel's central theme of the quest for love. While Suresh feels the warmth of human love in his brief affairs with Mona, her own words are significant: "I wonder if he'll ever find what he's looking for" (70). Ironically, Sheila's "freedom" culminates in the freedom for Suresh from the bonds of flesh. Suffering, dealt with by the Buddha in *The Fire Sermon,* appeals to Suresh (130). Pain and suffering culminate in death which is the path to eternity. The spirit can realize its potentialities only when it frees itself from the pressure of will. Hence the reference to suicide as prescribed by Schopenhauer for the final release (131, 164). In T.S. Eliot's *The Dry Salvages,* the bone prays to Death, its God, for the final release into Eternity—a state of timelessness. As Eliot says, under the influence of *Bhagavad Gita*:

> But to apprehend
> The point of intersection of the
> timeless
> With time, is an occupation for
> the saint—
> (*The Dry Salvages* 11.200-02)

Suresh's prayer is for a "quick release" into the state of timelessness wherein suffering and pain can be finally overcome and the unending bliss of love realized. As Lord Krishna says in *Bhagavad Gita,* "Whatever a man remembers at the last, when he is leaving the body will be realized in the hereafter." (Ch. VII, "The Way to Eternal Brahman"). The state of bliss can be attained by means of "self-surrender" to the Ultimate in order to realize the "Moment, the moment in and out of time" (*The Dry Salvages* 1.207). It is this "moment," the microcosmic form of "the timeless," which is central to the thought of both Eliot and Shiv Kumar under Bergson's influence. Suresh Gupta as philosopher and lover is in search of this "moment" like the lover in Robert Browning. He experiences what Eliot calls "a lifetime's death in love."

A major paradox of the novel consists in the interplay of emotion and intellect, of the deeply felt experience and rational stance. Both Suresh and Sunil are men of reason intensely swayed by emotions, even though Sunil would like to call himself a "detective." Suresh's quest for ideal love leads to "pain that is painless and motionless" (*The Dry Salvages*). His anguish thus reaches the point of stillness. In fact, an intensely emotional experience, whether of love or anything else, sends one into a state of depression and disgust bordering on philosophical resignation. Hence Suresh's frequent expression of the word "Karma."

In one of his letters from Elmira, Suresh says:

> Imagine the duality of my consciousness. I have now begun to feel as if every idea swung on parallel bars: the abstract philosophical truth and its corresponding corporeal manifestation in actual life. Or, is it my pain that has given me this double vision? (127)

This explains the paradoxical nature of Suresh. In spite of his frequent lapsing into emotional excitement and philosophical abstraction, he is perfectly rational in his diligent pursuit to expose Shells's adventure at The Snow Cap, culminating in the final confrontation. But the supra-rational experience of Suresh, a being gifted with intuitive perception confuses the narrator, Sunil Sharma, the self-conscious academic, who feels he can make anyone his "victim." On the contrary, he falls a victim to himself while encountering a superior intellect in Suresh. In fact, Sunil, in spite of all his self-glorification as a 'detective', is able to track down the sexual adventures of Sheila more on account of chance encounters (whether at the lake or at Dehra Doon) than the ratiocination and relentless pursuit of a sleuth. However, despite his shortcomings his character has its own interest for the reader. Shiv Kumar's use of the detective-story method is a result of the presence in him of what W.K. Wimsatt would call the "exceptional power of analysis as opposed to the merely creative talent." The reveries that the narrator at times slides into remind us of the abstractions of Edgar Allan Poe's famous reasoner C. Auguste Dupin. Poe in "The Purloined Letter" refers to the intuitive/poetic faculty that enables the reasoner to rise above the average mental level in perceiving connections between the apparently discordant elements. This is the ability, to quote the narrator of *The Bone's Prayer,* "to recall, interblend and harmonize all disparate elements into a pattern" (78). Sunil Sharma's "self-communication" and "passive, neutral mode of contemplation" (24) regarding love, philosophy, and music give to the narrative the tone of an interior monologue. This is in keeping with his contemplation on death and his attempts at communicating with the spirit of Suresh in the initial chapters. From that point onwards, the entire narrative is rendered in terms of a memory, an intensely realized emotional experience of a tragedy. The poet in Shiv K. Kumar is also palpable in the evocation of an atmosphere of beauty and meditative calm achieved by means of a series of symbolic details spread over the narrative. Thus Krishna teaching *Gita* to Arjuna, the "Holi Grail," the Swamiji, and the grotesque nightmare are suggestive.

The "double vision" that Suresh refers to characterizes the paradoxical nature of the novel itself. An exquisite irony pervades the rendition of character and incident, bringing on the basic tension in the novelist's vision of life. While taking the reader into the realm of the profoundest philosophy,—a synthesis of the teaching of *Bhagavad Gita,* Schopenhauer, the Buddha, and Bergson—the novelist is at once down-to-earth in his commonsense attitude to life. The novel is devastating in its exposure of superstition and false religious propaganda in the contemporary India. The device of the first-person narration by a confidant of the central character adds significance to the novel's ironic dimension. The banter is evident in the references to the happenings at the Chandi temple (like the animal sacrifice). At this point the novelist draws a significant comparison between the sacrificial lamb and Sheila's husband R.P. Mohan brought by her to the temple on their way for honeymoon at Bikrata, her former rendezvous (148). Even the priests ("the butchers") who fleece the devotees cannot escape the scourge. The description of the Transcendental Meditation session, conducted by Maharaj Swami Shantanandaji is interesting (Ch. XV). The peace-seekers attending the sessions are "tax-dodgers, corrupt bureaucrats, disgruntled politicians and, of course, young men"(83). Some of the young men attend the sessions more to enjoy the beauty of the girls in "meditation" than to experience any higher religious ecstasy. The "tomfoolery, that Suresh notices there *remains* one of the goings-on at the modern "ashrams" in urban areas where even sexual perversions are preached as spiritual experience. In contrast to all this "humbuggery," Suresh's quest is for a religion of the heart. As in T.S. Eliot, in Shiv K. Kumar too, it is not superstition but religious humanism that determines the writer's attitude to life.

Unlike Raja Rao, who in *The Serpent and the Rope* leaves the reader confused in a web of "Maya," Shiv Kumar brings him closer to the realities of everyday life, at the same time offering him glimpses of abstract thought. While exposing the sham in contemporary society with an ironic vision, he is different from R.K. Narayan in presenting the deepest personal tragedies of men and women in terms of a poetic experience. Like many an Indian English novelist, Shiv K. Kumar too is concerned with the East-West encounter both in the spiritual and mundane aspects. Just as the philosopher-protagonists in Raja Rao's *The Serpent and the Rope* and Bhattacharya's *A Dream in Hawaii* go on a voyage to the West, so also Suresh Gupta in Shiv K. Kumar's novel has his inevitable journey to the West, arranged by his friend. Suresh's longing for love in his affair with Caroline Gunther receives a rebuff when she runs away with the American guitarist, giving him the damning cultural shock. His class-room discussions convince him of the "impossible task of smuggling a bit of India into this alien milieu" (127). And he feels helpless in the "crazy Western World" where there is little difference between *Bhagavad Gita* and *Kamasutra.* Caroline's mother warns her of the "incongruity" of her relationship with Suresh, the brown man. His predicament is summed up in one of his letters to Sunil: "...I seem to be constantly shuttling back and forth between two contending poles, seeking some intermediate point of rest at which I may realize true peace and happiness" (173). Death itself is to be such an "intermediate point of rest" for him.

The novelist throws light on a distressing aspect of the contemporary Indian situation resulting from Westernization when he exposes the behaviour of the ultra-modern girls like Sheila on the campus and outside of it—"The new type, Sir, you know, with the brains too," as Abdul Hamid Khan, the waiter at The Snow Cap quips (69). Ironically, it is in the call-girl Mona that Suresh experiences the warmth of human love so conspicuously absent in the more respectable creatures like Sheila and Caroline.

Swami Yogananda, the professor-turned-yogi in Bhattacharya's *A Dream in Hawaii,* in his quest for "reality behind the appearances which were *maya,* the stuff of illusion," (8) goes to Hawaii to preach Indian philosophy to the Americans. His own sensual yearnings and excitement at the sight of "the body's bareness" leave him disenchanted. Suresh, on the contrary, is a class-room teacher with no such pretensions to uplift mankind and lives the very experience of the reality taught in the Eastern and Western philosophical systems. In both *A Dream in Hawaii* and *The Bone's Prayer* the conclusion is thoughtful. Swami Yogananda's disenchantment with the life in Hawaii makes him run back to India with a shattered dream. The journey of Suresh's body is to "the other world," the spiritual India, which is the reality behind the "Maya" that is modern Western life. Thus both the novelists raise questions of far-reaching significance concerning the East-West encounter.

The irony of Shiv Kumar is directed not only against Westernization but the basic hypocrisy of the Indian system. Even though he is not concerned with the lives of the princes or of paupers like Manohar Malgaonkar or Mulk Raj Anand, he nevertheless comments on the human situation within the limits of his own concerns. He not only exposes the sham that is in the lives of the over-sophisticated girls like Sheila but laughs at the hierarchical gradation in the sectors of Chandigarh, inhabited by upper class people like Dutt, the "little god from sector one" (32). The centrifugal existence of the Chandigharians confined to their respective sectors dehumanizes them. These individuals, living in their cocoons, form themselves into some sort of caste system. In addition to these, the novelist's comments on social evils like adultery, prostitution (50, 67) and animal sacrifice (143) show his deep concern for human values.

In fact, what is ultimately significant in *The Bone's Prayer* is the novelist's comment on the human situation in general. The novel deals with not only love between man and woman but the tender attachment of sons and mothers, of friends, and of pets and masters. The vital need of life is stated in unmistakable terms in the words of the narrator: "A smile, a gesture of the hand, a flicker of the eyelids, a peculiar modulation of the voice—these are the things that make one human and real" (106). Sunil Sharma's concern for his distressed friend is simply amazing. His attachment to his mother, the servant boy Vacchas, and the dog Zeus speaks for the novelist's zest for life. Zeus is symbolic of the unsullied faith which is sometimes doubtful in man.

The Bone's Prayer is thus multi-dimensional in its significance, each level of its meaning gradually unfolding itself before the reader as he goes through it. Like a symbol it lends itself to multiple interpretation and defies an easy classification as a metaphysical novel or a sociological novel.

While containing the several elements common to the Indo-English novels, like the East-West question, philosophical quest and Indian myth, it goes beyond these in the complexity of its theme and dexterity of the presentation, coming close to the business and bosoms of the moderns.

11

TECHNIQUE IN THE SHORT STORIES OF TAGORE*

I

While Rabindranath Tagore's international reputation rests largely on his poetry, his short stories too have brought him considerable recognition as one of the foremost Indian writers. Perhaps the short story form, on account of its brevity and unity of effect, has served him as a powerful vehicle for conveying his insight into different facets of human experience. His multi-dimensional vision of life is discernible in the sixty one short stories he has written. In them significant moments in human life are depicted, telescoping man's relationship with man and with environment.

Tagore's short stories have received some critical attention over the years. Nirmal Kumar Sidhanta has surveyed them in both the thematic and the technical aspects.[1] This survey, however, by its very nature, tends to be too diffuse to focus on the technique of his short story. C.V. Venugopal makes a brief mention of Tagore's achievement in the context of the Indian short story in English.[2] G.D. Khanolkar, in his biography of Tagore, gives us the facts about the birth of the short story in Tagore's writing.[3] However, it might be profitable to take into account Tagore's own views on the short story form and to analyze a few representative stories in an attempt to assess the extent to which he is able to put into practice his own principles.

As G.D. Khanolkar tells us, Tagore's short stories "took their birth from his peregrinations," (96) through his estates.

* *Kakatiya Journal of English Studies*, Vol. I, 1976, 73-92.

At Shileida, Patisar or Shahazadpur Tagore would freely mix with the peasant folks and listen to them for hours as a confidante. He would record all that he had observed in the simple men during the course of the day. In a letter from Shahazadpur he says:

> So often I feel I could write lots of little stories—lovely ones. I would enjoy writing them. Sometimes all sorts of feelings flit through my head, too many to put into verse. They have to be put into diaries and such like (97).

These feelings subsequently took the shape of "secret tales" or "short stories." Thus what Tagore did in the stories was to record certain moments in the lives of the simple rustics and townsmen as distinct from the highly sophisticated men of the city. In these short stories, he aims at a certain degree of concreteness of presentation with social and psychological realism. In this context he questions the contemporary reviewers, saying, "they pay to my short stories only a fraction of the regard they pay to my poetry, songs and plays." And he tells us that "To read them, brings back my travels as a young man along the rivers, and recaptures the happiness I derived in the villages from both Man and Nature. Even in this my old age, my heart relives those happy days, and my spirit leaps for joy" (99). However, this statement need not be read as meaning that Tagore felt "poetic" rapture, in those village scenes he had in mind. Generally critics have a tendency to ignore the realistic aspects of the tales, reading them only as poetic effusions. In fact, Tagore himself has asserted:

> Anybody who calls my stories "lyrical" simply shows that he is out of touch with reality (98).

The reality that is represented in his works is neither naturalistic crudeness nor sheer poetic fancy. In fact, it is the everyday reality brought close to the mind and heart of the reader by the genius of a poet. This is made clear by Tagore himself while describing the way he composed short stories during the monsoon when he was somewhat free from the estate work:

> I am sitting, writing a story, slowly and steadily. The light and shade of the world outside, its colours and voices, are mingling in my pen. The world I am fashioning, with

> all its inhabitants, is set about with this very sun and rain, this flowing river and its reedy islands, this monsoon sky and this shaded village, this rice-field standing so thick in its ever-gurgling water. Thus reality and beauty pass inescapably into my writings—and yet my reader can never fully share them. If I could only set down in my stories, just as it is, all that I see and feel—this river glowing in the lovely, laughing, cloud-free monsoon sunshine; the trees and creepers on her banks; the untroubled peace that they scatter over the hamlets—then would my reader wittingly confess, be it only for an instant, the living reality of it all; he would call it, no poet's fancy, but a picture true to life (100).

Thus there is in Tagore an urge to mingle with the world of beauty as well as with the world of the living human beings with all their happiness and misery, successes and failures.

Khanolkar maintains: "There is no room in his short stories for politics and social problems for which his chosen vehicle was to be the novel" (100). While there is no room for politics in Tagore's short stories, some of them like "Babus of Nayanjore," "The Cabuliwallah" and "Mashi" do touch the social and personal problems. However, he is not a social reformer in the commonly accepted sense of the term. In fact, as Tagore himself explains in one of his letters from Shileida dated 27 June 1894, the happy thought has suddenly come into his head that instead of trying to improve the world and failing, he might set himself to accomplishing what he can do, namely, write stories.[4]

Another interesting feature of Tagore's conception of the short story is the exquisite commingling of character with environment. This is stated in his letter of the 28th June 1895:

> As I sit writing bit by bit a story for *Sadhana,* the lights and shadows and colours of my surroundings mingle with my words. The scenes and characters and events that I am now imagining have this sun and rain and river, and the reeds on the river-bank, this monsoon sky, this shady village, these rain-nourished happy corn-fields to serve as their background and to give them life and reality (165).

Concerning the life-likeness of his characters, Tagore writes from Shileida:

> If I do nothing else but write short stories, I am happy and I make a few readers happy. The main cause of happiness is that people about whom I write become my companions: they are with me when I am confined to my room in the rain, on a sunny day they move about with me on the bright banks of the Padma.[5]

Thus in both the statements Tagore envisages a deep sense of harmony between character and environment.

My aim in this paper is to examine Tagore's short stories from the point of view of man's affinity with environment, character-analysis, and the manipulation of the openings and conclusions as devices in his narrative strategy.

II

Short stories like "Subha" and "The Auspicious Vision" are superb achievements in what Tagore himself says in his letter of the 28th June 1895 concerning the harmony of character and environment.[6] The characters of Subha and the dumb girl in "The Auspicious Vision" are a part of the very rhythm of Nature.

The story of "Subha," rendered in omniscient narration, fully brings out the fusion of character and environment. In the environment of her own family, the dumb Subha feels out of place, "a silent weight upon the heart of her parents." This makes her move away from her people and live in her own private world, getting desire to the silent and amiable Nature. The "illimitable loneliness" of the "silent troubled girl" Subha is the very loneliness of Nature:

> Nature, herself at full moon, like lonely Subha, was looking down on the sleeping earth. Her strong young life beat within her; joy and sadness filled her being to its brim; she reached the limits even of her own illimitable loneliness, nay, passed beyond them.[7]

The conclusion of the story, while it comes with a degree of suddenness to the husband of Subha, does not bring any surprise to the reader. On the contrary, it enhances the feeling that Subha, the dumb companion of the cows, the goats, and the kitten, cannot, alter all fit into the artificial world of the city-bred man. Subha should remain the darling of Nature, a part of Nature's eternal loneliness.

"The Auspicious Vision" is the story of a dumb village girl confronted by a sophisticated young man, Kantichandra. This story, like "Subha," depicts character in relation to environment and the tension or absence of it, consequent upon reversal of situation.

Kantichandra goes to the swamp of Nydighi for hunting and notices a village maiden whose "beauty had a rare freshness—as if she had just come from Vishwakarma's workshop"(50). Having been captivated by the beauty of the girl he goes to the house of her father Nabin Banerji and asks the old brahmin to give "Subha" in marriage to him. By an accident, Kantichandra mistakes the dumb girl for "Subha" her sister and finds himself married to the sister instead. He realizes the deception only at the time of the "Auspicious Vision" in the course of the wedding ceremony. However, on knowing that he really has not married the dumb girl for whom he approached Nabin, he feels "a sigh of intense relief, as of escape from calamity" (58).

Thus Kantichandra suddenly removes her from his mind. What was once a blissful vision of beauty vanishes from his mind. But the beauty of the dumb girl is a part of the eternal beauty of Nature. She is but "the companion of all the animals and birds of the locality" (58). Hence she has to remain a part of her environment.

"The Hungry Stones" opens with the narrator's account of a train journey during which he comes across a stranger, who tells the story later in the waiting-room. Thus the major part of the story is narrated by the stranger, the "extraordinary companion." The double narrator device gives dramatic objectivity and intensity to the story. The description of the "lonely" pleasure resort of the Emperor Shah II, the "solitary marble palace," is in tune with the state of the narrator "oppressed with solitude." The desert place weighs upon the narrator "like a nightmare" and exerts "a weird fascination" upon him. In fact, he feels as if the whole house is "like a living organism slowly and imperceptibly digesting me by the action of some stupefying gastric juice."[8] The wind around is "Laden with an oppressive scent." The setting sun is "a long dark curtain" falling upon the stage of the day. The narrator's mental framework makes him see visions: "methought I saw a bevy of joyous maidens coming down the steps to bathe in *Susta* in that summer evening" (7).

Having so far built up an atmosphere of suspense and fear, the author takes us into the realm of poetic fancy with the "mystic forms" brushing past the narrator and giving him the feeling that "it was the Muse that had taken advantage of my solitude and possessed me" (9). The narrator exclaims at the spirit's voice: "O lovely ethereal apparition! Where didst thou flourish and when? By what cool spring, under the shade of what date—groves, wast thou born in the lap of what homeless wanderer in the desert?"(19). But he is constantly brought back to the world of reality by the refrain of the crazy Meher Ali's scream: "Stand back! Stand back!! All is false! All is false!!" (20).

Thus the initial atmospheric build-up taking the reader into the medieval world and stirring up the emotion of fear is at variance with the delightful poetic fancy that is subsequently developed. The story falls between the two stools of depressing fear and poetic fancy. The character is out of tune with the environment, leaving the reader somewhat confused as to the ultimate effect of the tale.

III

In stories like "Mashi," "The Cabuliwallah," "Babus of Nayanjore," "The Elder Sister," and "The Home-coming," character acquires independent significance. These tales can be called tales of character.

"Mashi," presented largely in dialogue form, at once brings out the character of the aunt, Mashi, with her concern for Jotin. We also get a glimpse into Jotin's tenderness of heart toward Mani and his feeling of helplessness, and even jealousy, and Mani's childish pranks to go to her parents for the *annaprashan* function in spite of anything. The dialogue is racy, giving dramatic significance to the story.

Mingled with dialogue are the poetic utterances of Jotin about the stars and his recollection of a village minstrel's song,[9] supported by the omniscient author's words:

> The stars glistened in the sky like tear-drops. Jotin bowed his head in gratitude to his life that was about to depart, and when Death stretched out his right hand towards him through the darkness, he took it in perfect trust (11).

These poetic touches, subtly blended with dialogue, achieve a rare emotional effect. However, authorial intrusion at times, telling the reader about the "co-operation" at least two for "small talk," (12) does not contribute to the dramatic objectivity of the narrative.

Despite such blemishes, "Mashi" with its quick dialogue and superb control, is an impressive reading. The conclusion, wherein Mani is brought to Jotin's feet, is particularly effective. Mashi emerges as the loving aunt, as the bridge between Jotin and Mani. While her concern to see that Mani stays with Jotin fully brings out her character as the loving aunt, Mani's father bringing her back to her husband deepens the family sentiment.

"Babus of Nayanjore" portrays the clash of values between the aristocracy and the middle class. Kailas Babu, personally amiable and friendly with everyone, represents a conflict within himself. He does not consciously clash with the middle class. Having been brought up in the "old-world Babus," his tragedy lies in his inability to shake off from the snobbery of the aristocracy. Despite the fact that at heart "he is the most modest of men," he is extravagant, taking enormous pains to exhibit his "family pride." This, however, finally lands him in trouble with the narrator and his friends.

If Kailas Babu is extravagant, the narrator is self-conscious, being proud of his middle-class status. That is the reason for his dislike of Kailas Babu. He is immodest too, when he says that "among the young men of Bengal I was regarded by parents generally as a very eligible match."[10] His middle-class pride is baseless since he can imagine as his bride only "a wealthy father's only daughter, extremely beautiful and highly educated." And he feels he "was so good" (181). Thus if Kailas Babu suffers under excessive family pride, the narrator suffers under self-consciousness. In fact, both of them have fallen victims to self-deception. What the narrator calls the old man's "arrogance" and "vanity" are attributes not absent in himself. Out of sheer spite for Thakur Dada, he plays a practical joke on the old man. And his vicarious pleasure drives the reader away from him and closer to Kailas Babu. But the remarkable thing about the narrator is the change in his character at the sobbing of Kailas Babu's grand daughter:

> All the ugliness of my cruelty rose up to condemn me. I slunk out of the room in silence, like a kicked dog (187).

In fact, Kusum has been the object of his attention. His arrogance is evident when he says:

> No thought had ever entered my mind that she would be a possible partner for my self. All the same, it seemed quite certain to me that some day or other Kailas Babu would offer her, with all due worship, as an oblation at my shrine (182).

And he readily proposes marriage with Kusum as though by means of deception he has achieved his objective.

Thus in this story there is clash of character and conflict of class values. Here is no natural simplicity and poetry of a Subha but only urban sophistication and trickery. Kailas Babu, despite his modesty and heart's affection, is out of tune with environment. The narrator, with his middle-class pride, nonetheless desires to marry a wealthy father's daughter.

Another story in which the first-person narrator is a participant in the events is "The Cabuliwallah." The initial paragraph establishes the character of Mini, the centre of attention for the Cabuliwallah and the narrator. Mini's innocence and childish pranks are fully realized in her questions about the elephant in the clouds and when she says, "Father! what relation is Mother to you?"

Mini's fascination for the Cabuliwallah is a matter of curiosity to the narrator: "And for me, this child's talk with a grown-up man had always in it something strangely fascinating" (261). Mini's mother would implore him to "beware of that man." An occasional suspicion lingers even in the narrator's mind as when he sees, "in the corner of a dark room, suddenly to surprise this tall, loose-garmented, much bebagged man"

(264). He is superstitious and does not want the Cabuliwallah, who has returned from the prison, to see the bride Mini. He even turns harsh when the Cabuliwallah takes out the little packet of almonds, raisins, and grapes as a gift to his old friend. While behaving like this, the narrator is, however, "a little sorry." And when the whole truth of the Cabuliwallah's sentiments dawns upon him,

> Tears come to my eyes. I forgot that he was a poor Cabuli fruit-seller, while I was.... But no, what was I more than he? He also was a father (270).

The narrator's experience makes him undergo psychological change till he finally turns to humaneness. Thus the story of "The Cabuliwallah" is notable for the portrayal of the three characters in relation to one another. Character here predominates over environment, making the story a remarkable study in human relationship.

An interesting short story depicting both human relationship and environment, the former predominating, is "The Postmaster." The Postmaster, a city-bred man, "felt like a fish out of water in this remote village."[11] As a silver lining to the dark cloud of this isolation comes his association with Ratan. When he is ill, Ratan nurses him back to health. While he revolts to the environment of Ulapur the only source of his peace is Ratan. The agony of impending separation is realized in dramatic terms:

> The master said: "You need not be anxious about my going away, Ratan: I shall , tell my successor to look after you."
>
> . . . .
>
> She burst out weeping, and said:
>
> "No, no, you need not tell anybody anything at all about me; I don't want to stay on here" (167).

When the boat carrying the Postmaster moves on the river, he intensely feels the relationship between the natural and the human:

> ...the grief-stricken force of a village girl seemed to represent for him the great unspoken pervading grief of Mother Earth herself (168).

While thus on the one hand the Postmaster is pulled by the sentiment he has developed for Ratan, on the other he is longing for "the nearness of mother and sister" (164). He rejects the rural Ulapur for the urban Calcutta but his affection for Ratan keeps him still attached to the land he has forsaken. Tagore has exquisitely brought out this conflict within the character of the Postmaster. But when he generalizes about the separation of Ratan and the Postmaster,..."inscrutable are the ways of a woman's heart!" (167) or exclaims at the end of the story, "Alas for the foolish human heart!" (169) the effect of the narrative gets somewhat diluted.

As in "The Cabuliwallah" and "Babus of Nayanjore," in "The Elder Sister" and "The Home-Coming" too the character undergoes gradual change from a state of disharmony to that of harmony.

In the opening paragraphs of "The Elder Sister" we are introduced to Sasikala as longing for her husband's return from abroad. The omniscient narrator probes into her mind and brings out all the delicate sentiments of a woman separated from her husband. Into this atmosphere comes the news of the birth of Nilmani to Sasi's parents, shattering the hopes of Sasi and Joygopal inheriting the property of Sasi's father. But when Nilmani's mother dies leaving the child in Sasi's care, her jealousy turns into intense love for the brother: "She surrendered herself completely to this wayward little tyrant" (127).

As the omniscient narrator says, "The greatest changes in a woman's nature are wrought by love; in a man's, by ambition" (129). Sasi's attempts to save Nilmani from the cruelty of Joygopal resulting in the separation of husband and wife, bring Sasi's character to full development. Leaving the boy in the custody of the Magistrate, Sasi meets her husband in "that old, ever familiar house." The meeting here is a contrast to the first meeting which is preceded by sweet memories. It is, in short, a meeting suggestive of permanent separation: "The decree of Prajapati!"

In "The Home-Coming," Phatik is presented as a naughty boy, an innocent and mischievous child of the rural environment. In spite of his initial happiness to go to Calcutta with his uncle, once he is in the city he feels like a "fish out of water" as the Postmaster does in Ulapur. Phatik's story symbolizes man's inseparableness from environment. Here is a contrast between two cultures—the rural and the urban—the one simple and endearing and the other complex and alienating. Phatik undergoes physical change, his voice growing "hoarse" and his face growing "suddenly angular and insightly." The author shows how Phatik's tragedy lies in his inability to adjust to a new environment into which he willingly goes and out of which he struggles tragically to emerge.

Within the brief space of the short story Tagore is able to achieve superb characterization. His characters sometimes embody his ideal of the harmony of character and environment. Characters like Subha and Kanti's bride in "The Auspicious Vision" are a part of the very rhythm of the natural life. But once the character is exposed to an alien environment, there is breakdown of communication.

Subha is dismissed for being dumb and Kanti's bride becomes an object of his hatred. The tragedy of Phatik in "The Home-Coming" is this inability of the character to break off from the environment in which he is brought up. Kailas Babu's tragedy is a result of the artificial values he has developed, standing between the two worlds of the "old-world" Babus and the middle class.

Sometimes a sudden change in the character is presented. In the midst of his rejoicing at the predicament of Kailas Babu following the practical joke, the narrator is confronted by Kusum's pathetic appeal. A sense of remorse overtakes him. Sasikala in "The Elder Sister" is changed from jealousy for the infant brother into intense love for him, going to the extent of permanently alienating her own husband.

While characters like Subha and the dumb girl in "The Auspicious Vision" bring out the closeness of the human world with the natural, others like Mashi bring out the domestic relationship. Kusum and the Cabuliwallah portray a wider human relationship.

Thus the range of Tagore's characterization is personal as well as social, giving width to his artistry without sacrificing depth. The majority of his characters are simple folks like

Subha, the village Postmaster, and Ratan, or Phatik the village boy, and through them as realized in their environment Tagore visualizes that "principle of unity" which he says, is "the true principle of art."[12] In his short stories he normally avoids the affluent and the urbanized characters. Behind this choice is an artistic concern on his part to study man as being basically an inseparable part of the unity of existence. In conformity with what Tagore says in his letter of June 28, 1895 concerning the origin of his short stories,[13] we have another of his statements regarding the kind of simple life that he is concerned with:

> I do not seek to glorify poverty. But simplicity is of greater price than the appendages of luxury. The simplicity of which I speak is not merely the effect of a lack of superfluity: it is one of the signs of perfection. When this dawns on mankind, the unhealthy fog which now besmirches civilization will be lifted. It is for lack of this simplicity that the necessaries of life become so rare and costly.[14]

IV

Tagore takes great care to establish the subject of his story in his openings. The narrator, first-person participant or omniscient author, makes certain explicit statements that impinge on the reader's mind and at once pull him into the flow of events. E.A. Poe achieves this to a high degree in the opening paragraph of "The Fall of the House of Usher." Wayne C. Booth calls this "mood-building." In the words of Professor Booth:

> Every adjective and detail intended to set our mood is a part of the growing mood and experience of the central character; the rhetoric now seems functional, "intrinsic."[15]

Tagore achieves this "mood-building" in the openings of some of the short stories like "The Hungry Stones." The narrator meets the stranger in the train, who exclaims: "There happen more things in heaven and earth, Horatio, than are reported in your newspapers."[16] And from a reference to certain "secret and unheard-of forces" at work, we are led into the mysterious events of the story narrated by the stranger. In some of the openings a certain character is established. In "The

Cabuliwallah," we are given a glimpse into Mini's character. In "The Home-Coming," Phatik's character is established, but the final events, of course, give an unexpected turn to the character. In the opening paragraphs of "Subha," the author brings out the ironic implications of Subha's character. However, the opening of "The Elder Sister" does not effectively establish any character or event. In "The Skeleton," the reader is taken to the skeleton which would "rattle in the breeze." But the subsequent events do not produce any emotional effect on the reader. The dialogue between the narrator and the spirit of the beautiful widow does not create an effect of fear indicated by the narrator's "Fancy of my sleepless, excited brain."[17] While there is an attempt on the author's part to comment on the futility of physical beauty, the mixing of "delight" and fancy of the "sleepless, excited brain" produces a somewhat ludicrous effect. The conclusion does not go well with the beginning.

"Mashi," in its development on the lines of a drama, opens with a dialogue between Mashi and Jotin at once bringing out the three characters. And the conclusion logically fits well with the opening in its dramatic effect. In "The Home-Coming," the opening gives us Phatik as a mischievous boy but the conclusion presents him in a tragic situation. Whereas the opening is a statement by the omniscient author, the conclusion dramatizes the situation.

The dramatic presentation of a situation revealing character as opposed to telling by the author is what Caroline Gordon and Allen Tate mean when, referring to Poe's "The Fall of the House of Usher," they view the story as a step in the progress toward mastery of *"creative, active* detail which came into this tradition of fiction with Flaubert, to be perfected later by James, Chekhov, and Joyce."[18] While in some of the stories like "The Hungry Stones" and "Subha," there is an attempt at manipulating the reader's mood, in some like "Mashi," there is the "*creative, active* detail" of the tradition of Flaubert and Chekhov that Gordon and Tate refer to.

The conclusions of some of the tales by the skilful manipulation of character and incident come upon the reader with a fine suddenness. In "Subha," the conclusion is sudden, particularly for the husband when he realizes that he was after all deceived. But it does not come to the reader with the same effect. In this regard "My Fair Neighbour" is exquisitely rendered. The self-deception on the part of the narrator is revealed in the opening itself:

> Even my nearest intimate, Nabin, knew nothing of the real state of my mind. And I had a sort of bride that I could keep my passion pure by thus concealing it in the inmost recesses of my heart.[19]

With Nabin "as a screen," writing poetry in the name of Nabin, "a true warmth of feeling gushed out into these vicarious poems" about the fair neighbour, the widow. And the narrator's self-deception is brought to completion with the sudden revelation that Nabin's bride is the very fair neighbour worshipped in his poems. The conclusion is as sudden to the character himself as it is to the reader. An equally effective conclusion is that of "The Elder Sister" that after all Sasi has to pay with her life for her affection for the brother.

The foregoing analyses of a few of Tagore's well-known short stories have brought to light some interesting artistic features. While the writer eminently succeeds in achieving a synthesis of character and environment in stories like "Subha" and "The Auspicious Vision," in others like "Hungry Stones," "Babus of Nayanjore" and "The Home-Coming," character is at variance with environment. Some of the stories like "Mashi," "The Cabuliwallah," and "The Elder Sister" are excellent studies in character-development. "Mashi" is particularly dramatic, the dialogue revealing nuances of character. Furthermore, what makes the stories so striking is the way the author opens and concludes them, keeping the reader fully engrossed in the narrative. However, in some of the stories like "The Postmaster" and "Mashi" the craftsmanship suffers because of the author's overt comments.

NOTES

1. Nirmal Kumar Sidhanta, "*Rabindranath's Short Stories,*" *Rabindranath Tagore, 1861-1961: A Centenary Volume* (New Delhi: Sahitya Akademi, 1961) 276-92.
2. C.V. Venugopal, "The Indian Short Story in English: A Survey," *The Banasthali Patrika,* No. 12 (January, 1969) 98-104.

3. G.D. Khanolkar, *The Lute and the Plough: A Life of Rabindranath Tagore.* Trans. Thomas Gay (Bombay: The Book Centre Private Ltd., 1963) 96-100. Hereafter textual references are given in parentheses.
4. Somnath Maitra, "The Letters of Rabindranath Tagore," *Rabindranath Tagore,* 1861-1961: *A Centenary Volume,* 165. Hereafter textual references are given in parentheses.
5. Quoted in Nirmal Kumar Sidhanta 277.
6. Somnath Maitra.
7. Rabindranath Tagore, *Mashi and Other Stories* (London: Macmillan and Co. Limited, 1966) 152. Hereafter referred to as *Mashi and Other Stories.* Textual references are given in parentheses.
8. Rabindranath Tagore, *Hungry Stones and other Stories* (London: Macmillan and Co. Limited, 1916) 6. Hereafter referred to as *Hungry Stones and other Stories.* Textual references are given in parentheses.
9. *Mashi and other Stories* 9.
10. *Hungry Stones and other Stories* 181.
11. *Mashi and other Stories* 160.
12. Prithwish Neogy, ed. *Rabindranath Tagore on Art and Aesthetics* (Calcutta: Orient Longmans, 1961) 21.
13. Somnath Maitra 165.
14. *The Centre of Indian Culture* (Calcutta: Visva Bharati, 1962) 7.
15. Wayne C. Booth, *The Rhetoric of Fiction* (Chicago: The University of Chicago Press, 1961) 202.
16. *Hungry Stones and Other Stories* 3.
17. *Mashi and other Stories* 32.
18. Caroline Gordon and Allen Tate, *The House of Fiction* (New York: Charles Scribner's Sons, 1950) 116.
19. *Mashi and Other Stories* 215.

12

From Darkness to Light: V.S. Naipaul's Indian Odyssey

The Swedish Academy's citation for the Nobel Prize to V.S. Naipaul in December 2001 said that he was given the award "for having united perceptive narrative and incorruptible scrutiny in works that compel us to see the presence of suppressed histories."[1] While scrutinizing the several suppressed Third World histories, Naipaul has been rediscovering his own ancestral Indian civilization. Certainly India has a special place in his mind. In his acceptance speech, Naipaul said: "I was an intuitive writer. That was so, and that remains so now, when I am nearly at the end...I had to do the books I did because there were no books about those subjects. I had to clear up my world, elucidate it, for myself...."[2] Naipaul's quest over the decades has been for his own self. What is unique about the travel books dealing with his peregrinations across the continents has been his scrutiny of men and matters with an eagle-like sharp vision. The traveller's curiosity to explore new cultures is coupled with the novelist's idealizing instinct.

Referring to Naipaul as a traveller, Leon Gottfield says:

> But it has another kind of power—the power of an encounter of a subtle, well-trained, individualistic mind with forces going beyond the verge of the comprehensible, where a sense of righteousness, religious revivalism, the rage of the dispossessed, and the dreams of an ideal state merge and boil. Naipaul finds few answers to his many questions. After all, however, it is not the arrival but the journey that matters.[3]

Naipaul's continuing travels to the enigma that is India have been his attempts at an "arrival" in the course of his search for an ancestral culture that has given him inner strength, an "arrival" different from the one in England.

In his Foreword to *India: A Wounded Civilization,* Naipaul says: "India is for me a difficult country. It isn't my home and cannot be my home; and yet I cannot reject it or be indifferent to it; I cannot travel only for the sights. I am at once too close and too far."[4] Nevertheless, he is not caught in "a love-hate relationship with Hinduism,"[5] as John Thieme puts it. In fact, he is engaged in coming to terms with the idea or reality that is Hindu India. Having heard of the ancient civilization of the country of his forefathers, Naipaul visited India for the first time in 1962. And the visit led to the writing of the controversial book *An Area of Darkness.* At Port of Spain in Trinidad he had been watching the Hindu rituals in his family with ironic detachment. On his first visit to the country from where his family customs and traditions originated, he was appalled by the squalor and poverty as well as hypocrisy, political corruption, and official apathy around. His adverse reaction to such a state of affairs might be typical of a Westerner used to affluence, tidy surroundings, time sense, less of apathy on official levels. Indians might generally take the state of affairs for granted. Basic to Naipaul's sense of shock had been his concern for the plight of common man. Despite decades of independence, the detestable aspects of public life in the country questioned by Naipaul still persist. To Rahul Singh's question during his visit to India after the award of the Nobel Prize why he had been so harsh on India in his first two books on the country, Naipaul said: "I had no distaste for India...It was personal anguish. I was expecting to be terrified." And he added: *"An Area of Darkness* had its impact on Indians, because they recognized the pain in which it was written and also recognised that what I was saying was true."[6] In his article "Naipaul's India and Mine," Nissim Ezekiel questions Naipaul, may be for some justifiable reasons.[7] But he is limited in his appraisal of Naipaul. The real Naipaul however, emerges only on a holistic assessment of the man and his writings, particularly in the light of his statements on *An Area of Darkness* during his recent visits to India and a rereading of the book.

In his Nobel Prize acceptance speech, Naipaul said, "I was surrounded by areas of darkness." These areas of darkness might be in the Third World countries he had been trying to explore or in his own psyche as an immigrant in the West with diasporic undulations. Leon Gottfield refers to the "personal complexity" of *An Area of Darkness,* "the darkness in India echoing the darkness within himself."[8] The real "darkness" is not necessarily the physical aspects of India—the poverty, filth, complacency, dishonesty, etc.—but a darkness in his own self which he has been trying to penetrate in his attempts to see the light coming down the ages.

Referring to Naipaul's non-fiction dealing with Third-World countries, Gita Hariharan says:

> Darkness rules. If there is light, it only exposes wounds. Mutinities abound (mutinees, revolts, insurgencies; not dissent or movement or struggle). In short, there is chaos; no spark, no ember of hope. And where are these chaotic 'half-worlds' Naipaul travels in with so much writerly pain and fear? All of them are, without exception, non-Western countries.... These areas of darkness serve as a perennial foil to the refined, cultured European ethos.[9]

Whatever the Westernized Naipaul's attitude to Africa and other Third-World countries generally, his reaction to the land of his ancestors has been different. He has been trying to see the light coming from ancient times through the haze. Hariharan distorts Naipaul's idea of India when she compares the "darkness" he sees in India with Joseph Conrad's "heart of darkness" in the Congo:

> Just as Conrad's European travellers 'glide like phantoms,' in Africa, 'cut off from the comprehension of (their) surroundings,' Naipaul too glides like a nervous, unhappy phantom across the prehistoric world *from the Congo to Bombay,* all generally places where 'the moist heat saps energy and will.'[10]

Such a generalization is untenable. In his essay "Conrad's Darkness," Naipaul calls non-Western countries "half-made." But he was aware of the fullness of the Indian culture, his "idea of India," distorted by changing circumstances. India has been a deep-seated emotional problem for him and he is still trying to fully comprehend the mystery.

In *Roots,* Alex Haley, a Black American, goes to Africa in search of the origin of his ancestor taken to America as a slave. Although a free American citizen now, Haley feels different from the white Americans. While Naipaul's Hindu Brahmin forefathers went to Trinidad from Uttar Pradesh in India as indentured labourers, Haley's African Negro forebears had been forcibly brought by the Whites to America as slaves. Naipaul's people did not get Creolised in Trinidad but preserved their Hindu Brahmin customs and traditions. Naipaul had been deeply attached to his family. His ironic detachment notwithstanding, he has been on a quest for his true self rooted in the ancestral culture in India from where the Hindu rituals and traditions practised by his elders at home in Port of Spain originated. It has indeed been a rediscovery of the cultural moorings that have made India a stable nation despite all the upheavals over the centuries. In fact, in *An Area of Darkness,* Naipaul regrets what he and his family in Trinidad have missed, living in an "alienness" into which they got absorbed:

> We knew that something which was once whole had been washed away. What was whole was the idea of India.
>
> To preserve this conception of India as a country still whole, historical facts had not been suppressed. They had been acknowledged and ignored; and it was only in India that I was able to see this as part of the Indian ability to retreat, the ability genuinely what was obvious: with others a foundation of neurosis, but with Indians only part of a greater philosophy of despair, leading to passivity, detachment, acceptance. It is only now, as the impatience of the observer is dissipated in the process of writing and self-inquiry, that I see how much this philosophy had also been mine. It had enabled me, through the stresses of a long residence in England, to withdraw completely from nationality and loyalties except to persons; it had made me content to be myself alone, my work, my name (the last two so different from the first); it had convinced me that every man was an island, and taught

> me to shield all that I knew to be good and pure within myself from the corruption of causes.[11]

Naipaul felt that even by the time of his first visit to India, the "philosophy of despair, leading to passivity, detachment, acceptance," had also been his on account of his ancestry. It is not what John Thieme calls "the vehement anti-Hinduism of *An Area of Darkness* and *India: A Wounded Civilization*"[12] but a recognition on Naipaul's part of the preeminence of the ancient Hindu civilization. He expressed the deep pain experienced by him on actually observing the way such a civilization was vandalized. Despite all the anger expressed in *An Area of Darkness,* Naipaul could recognize how the Indian would escape from the kind of neurosis that might break the Westerner under identical circumstances.

Philip Gourevitch refers to the concluding chapter in Naipaul's *The Enigma of Arrival* concerning death and human mystery and the author's recounting of the brief discourse by a distant-in-law on ancestral history at the time of his sister's funeral. Naipaul reminisces: "Men need history; it helps them to have an idea of who they are. But history, like sanctity, can reside in the heart; it is enough that there is something there."[13] In the course of his cultural explorations across the continents, with history in his heart, Naipaul looks back to his ancestral land as an answer to the spiritual problems of contemporary life.

As John Thieme says, "*The Mimic Men* was the first of his novels to be written after his traumatic journey to India: the journey described in his seventh book, *An Area of Darkness;* a journey that, it would seem, enabled him to understand that the roots of his detachment lay in his Hindu psyche; a journey that led him, in his quest to repudiate his Hindu background, to expose such detachment."[14] In his fiction, as in his non-fiction, it is not "repudiation" of Hindu background but a quest for his Hindu self that Naipaul is engaged in, as evident from his recent statements. For Ralph Singh, his Hindu self is inescapable. As he says:

> I no longer yearn for ideal landscapes and no longer wish to know the god of the city. This does not strike me as less. I feel, instead, I have lived through attachment

> and freed myself from one cycle of events. It gives me joy to find that in so doing I have also fulfilled the fourfold division of life prescribed by our Aryan ancestors. I have been student, householder and man of affairs, recluse.[15]

Unlike ending up with conflict as his characters like Ralph Singh, Ganesh or Biswas, Naipaul has been striving to achieve a resolution of the tension by means of his repeated visits to India and rethinking about the country.

During "At Home in the World: International Festival of Indian Literature" held in Neemrana Fort in Rajasthan in February 2002, when Nayantara Sahgal spoke about "Colonial Experience," Naipaul found her talk "too much" and said: "After 50 years of independence, what is the point? When did colonialism take place? Give a date. Without a date it is like dancing on air."[16] Naipaul's objection to the mention of "Colonial Experience" is understandable. As Bruce Bawer says, "At the center of Naipaul *oeuvre* lies a profound irony. It was Western colonialism that provided him with his first experiences of indignity and exploitation and planted in him a lifelong feeling of dislocation and an ire that continues to burn in his soul."[17] Naipaul has been striving to overcome the feeling of dislocation. He also found fault with Shashi Deshpande when she spoke about oppression of history and gender discrimination, saying "Banal words like gender discrimination irritate me. Words like oppression weary me."[18] His contempt for words like "oppression" and "colonialism" is on account of his concern for the contemporary India in relation to its hoary past. In the Epilogue to *In a Free State,* Naipaul says: "Perhaps that had been the only pure time, at the beginning, when the ancient artist, knowing no other land, had learned to look at his own and see it as complete."[19] It is the conservative Naipaul's nostalgia for a pure, Edenic moment in the past. As Malcolm Jones says, "He depicts colonialism and its aftermath. But he also sneers at the formerly colonized."[20] However, as his reaction during the recent meeting at Neemrana Fort makes it evident, Naipaul has recognized the adverse effects of colonialism on the Third World cultures. In the words of Stephen Schiff, Naipaul "was a scourge of the postcolonial world; an uncompromising critic of every liberation movement, every idealogue and revolutionary."[21] A child of the colony of Trinidad, he has come a long way from the conditions of oppression and colonialism. Instead of a postcolonial perspective, he has the historical as a source of inner strength, since he is engrossed with issues of ancestral origins. As he says in *A Way in the World,* "We cannot understand all the traits we have inherited. Sometimes we can be strangers to ourselves."[22]

Outside the formal sessions of the Neemrana meet, other Indian writers were said to have been apprehensive of facing Naipaul: "He does not suffer fools gladly and it's hard to tell who or what will irritate him." While Khushwant Singh was seen frequently in his company, other writers "kept a wary distance from the irascible Nobel Laureate, speaking only when he summoned them for a conversation."[23] This is due to Naipaul's famously forbidding, admonitory presence, what Saul Bellow called his "eagle-on-the-crags look" on his first meeting in London with Naipaul in the winter of 1982.[24] In his writings as well as his personal interaction with people, Naipaul is known as irascible and unpredictable. He has immense moral courage and intellectual honesty with unswerving literary integrity and a high degree of sophistication.

Jonathan Swift was called a misanthrope on account of the bitterness of his satire on mankind. But the bitterness was a result of his intense love for the humans and his desire to reform them. Naipaul's caustic criticism of human affairs, like Swift's, is basically on account of his concern for the people he encountered across the continents. In his "Prologue" to *Beyond Belief: Islamic Excursions Among the Converted Peoples,* Naipaul says that the writer of travel-books is "a discoverer of people, a finder-out of stories.... I began my career as a fiction writer, a manager of narrative; at that time I thought it the highest thing to be.... So in these travel books or cultural explorations of mine the writer as traveller steadily retreats; the people of the country come to the front; and I become again what I was at the beginning: a manager of narrative."[25] In his travel books, there is a unique blend of fact and fiction and the real people he encountered would sometimes look like fictional characters, just as the fictional characters in his novels would come alive as real people.

The "people" that Naipaul encountered provided the themes for his writings which were more than the pedestrian reporting of a journalist. As he says, "People are responding to the same political or religious and cultural pressures. The writer has only to listen very carefully and with a clear heart to what people say to him, and the next question, and the next."[26] In Naipaul's view, history is woven around people, it is a kind of order, despite occasional disorder. As Stephen Schiff says, "For him, the knowledge of history is a humanizing influence—humanizing in the sense of make humane."[27] Whether dealing with Africa and the Third World countries or the Caribbean, Naipaul's travel writings are imbued with such concern for the humane. He is intellectually competent and honest in his assessment of divergent cultures, past and present. As Naipaul tells Stephen Schiff,

> Writing isn't just being anti-African or anti-Negro—whatever. How on earth? It's absurd. The books have to look after themselves, and they will be around as long as people find that they are illuminating. Instead of coming to me asking "Why did you write this book?," you should be saying "How did you see so much?" That would be the question. And the question might be "Why did you have this eye—that you can point out the flaws in movements?" And I would say "It is easy to see the flaws in movements if you abolish sentimentality and you question everything that bothers you." Some people write simple things. The thing is, I am not a simple man. I have an interesting mind, a very analytical mind. And what I say tends to be interesting. Also very true. That's all that I can do about it. I can't lie. I can't served a cause. A cause always corrupts.[28]

This is indeed Naipaul's credo as a travel writer, forthright and without advocating any cause. Being intellectually honest and without narrow sentimentality, he eminently succeeds in analyzing men and matters with detachment.

While Khushwant Singh hailed the award of the Nobel Prize to Naipaul,[29] Gita Hariharan questioned it:

> Naipaul has been given the Nobel this year of all years. He has been given the Nobel in the midst of hawkish

> cacophony on the 'Clash of Civilizations' and growing prejudice against Muslims, indeed anyone of 'Middle Eastern appearance.' Naipaul has been given the Nobel soon after he has reacted to the September 11 tragedy, in myth-affirming terms, of Islam's calamitous effect on civilisation.[30]

For over five decades Naipaul has been commenting on human affairs in the same critical vein. Hariharan seems to appreciate Arundhati Roy's politics of "bombs and dams and globalization."[31] It is unfortunate that she not only sees politics in the award of the Nobel to Naipaul but also looks upon Arundhati Roy as a more important writer-activist. However, S. Prasannarajan, a journalist, is more convincing when he says: "In an age of writers as street performers of conscience-keeping, he (Naipaul) alone seems to see the vandalised national soul and he has the honesty to name the vandal-Islam."[32]

Naipaul looks with disdain at the Islamic culture from Iran to Indonesia. As he says in *Beyond Belief: Islamic Excursions Among the Converted Peoples,* "Converted peoples have to strip themselves of their past; of converted peoples nothing is required but the purest faith (if such a thing can be arrived at), Islam, submission. It is the most uncompromising kind of imperialism."[33] Naipaul's assertion is a result of his conviction that genuine cultural stability comes from a respect for the past. In the words of Khushwant Singh:

> Naipaul's *Among the Believers: An Islamic Journey* caused a lot of uneasiness among Muslims. Even Salman Rushdie accused him of harbouring anti-Muslim feelings. What Naipaul in fact wrote cannot be faulted. He observed that people who accepted Islam wrote off their pre-Islamic past. This phenomenon can be verified in Muslim countries today. In Egypt, the Pharaonic period which produced the pyramids, the Sphinx and many beautiful temples is only of historic interest, bringing in tourists and foreign exchange. It is the same in Pakistan. They have consigned their Hindu and Buddhist past to archives, museums and history books. Even the period of Sikh dominance is brushed aside as of little consequence. The destruction of

> the Buddhas in Baniyan is a recent example of erasing pre-Islamic past. This can be seen in all Muslim nations, including the most westernized like Turkey, Morocco and Tunisia. Naipaul did not invent this fact of history; he only exposed it.[34]

According to Malcolm Jones, Naipaul "reaffirmed his opinions regarding Islam at a reading in October 2001 in London, condemning what he called Islam's 'calamitous effect.'" Elaborating, Naipaul is reported to have said: "To be converted, you have to destroy your past, destroy your history. You have to stamp on it, you have to say, 'My ancestral culture does not exist, it doesn't matter.'"[35] Naipaul's views result from an unswerving faith in his own ancestral culture. Jones refers to "the cultural bankruptcy" that Naipaul chronicles and adds: "Rereading Naipaul now, in light of recent events, giving ourselves up to what the Swedish Academy called his 'incorruptible scrutiny," is to hear a dry, wise and illusionless voice whispering, 'Welcome to the world.'"[36]

Khushwant Singh recalls interviewing Naipaul (with Bhaichand Patel) for *Outlook* ("Hindu revivalists are mimicking Islamic fundamentalists," May 8, 2000) and says that the Nobel Laureate was heckled by him and Patel for what was widely believed to be the Sangh Parivar's view of the act of vandalism but "Naipaul stood his ground. He was an outside observer not concerned with the rights or wrongs of destroying a mosque. The phrase he used was explanatory: 'It was a balancing of history.' I interpreted this to imply that deep in the Hindu psyche was the resentment that Muslim invaders had destroyed hundreds of their temples. So what was devilish about destroying a dilapidated old mosque?"[37] What Khushwant Singh seems to appreciate in Naipaul is his dispassionate assessment of the Indian situation in the light of history. As a travel-writer, with his eagle-like sharp vision, he could observe the general resentment of the majority Hindus whose places of worship had been vandalised and who had been subjected to large-scale conversions by Islamic and Christian organizations by means of enticement and coercion. Such dubious methods of conversion had not been questioned by the opportunistic secularist politicians for more than half-a-century.

Naipaul's widening comprehension of the richness and complexity of the Indian civilization is evident. The "million mutinies" that he recognizes in the country have been resurgence of the Indian civilization that flourished even before the Western countries were civilized. As in *An Area of Darkness,* in *India: A Wounded Civilization* too he expresses agony at the chaos around. As he says:

> With Independence and growth, chaos and a loss of faith, India was awakening to its distress and the cruelties that had always lain below its apparent stability, its capacity simply for going on. Not everyone was content simply to have his being. The old equilibrium had gone, and at the moment all was chaos. But out of this chaos, out of the crumbling of the old Hindu system, and the spirit of rejection, India was learning new ways of seeing and feeling.[38]

Naipaul sees the wounds inflicted on the Indian civilization and the process of its recuperation. In *India: A Million Mutinies Now* he deals extensively with this process of Indian renaissance which is also Hindu resurgence. Industrialization and economic growth in India, as in any other country, have resulted in loss of traditional values. As Naipaul says: "Men honoured only money now. The great investment in development over three or four decades had led only to this: to 'corruption,' to the 'criminalization of politics.' In seeking to rise, India had undone itself. No one could be sure of anything now; all was fluid. Policeman, thief, politician—the roles had become interchangeable. And with money—the money of which the crowded, ugly skyscraper towers of Bombay spoke—many long-buried particularities had been released. These disruptive, lesser loyalties—of region, caste, and clan—now played on the surface of Indian life."[39] In these few sentences Naipaul has described the ills that continue to plague the Indian society despite all the technological advancement and economic growth. But he could understand the erosion of moral and spiritual values and observe the reaction of the common people. As he says, he grew up in Trinidad with two ideas of India: the private and personal, the India or the anxiety about where the migrant-Indians had come from was like a neurosis. And the second idea of India was one of the independence movement, the India of the great civilization and the great classical past. This second idea, Naipaul says, was an aspect of their identity, the community identity they had developed in the multi-racial Trinidad (7-8). When he first visited India in 1962 with that identity, he felt shattered on seeing the actual conditions prevailing in India. Despite political and bureaucratic corruption and castist and communal conflicts, Naipaul sees the new confidence of people, new identities. He finds a vibrant democracy despite the multiplicity of castes and communities. The effects of industrialization and green revolution are evident, notwithstanding the Naxalite movement confined to small pockets in the sprawling country. He could also observe the active brahmin—Hindu culture and resentment against anti-brahminism in the South. He is reminded of the pujas done at home in Port of Spain and the ceremonial readings from the epics and the scriptures (209). As Naipaul says:

> Through all the twists and turns of history, through all the imperial venturings in this part of the world, which that Portuguese arrival in India portended, and finally through the unlikely British presence in India, a Hindu India had grown again, more complete and unified than any India in the past. (143)

Whatever the hue and cry raised by the Liberal fans of Naipaul, his conviction since the beginnings of his visits to India has been unswerving.

In *The Clash of Civilizations and the Remaking of World Order,* Samuel P. Huntington argues that the "rivalry of the superpowers is replaced by the clash of civilizations." While identifying six or seven civilizations, Huntington perceives a clash between the two proselytizing religions of Christianity and Islam.[40] These proselytizing religions have taken undue advantage of the tolerance of the more ancient civilization of Hinduism in India. In the present "clash of civilizations" on the subcontinent, India is poised to regain much of the cultural richness which is the real source of intellectual and spiritual strength for the country now emerging as a global power. Despite occasional discordance, the multicultural India with its diverse religions is unified on account of the majority

Hindu concept of tolerance and universal brotherhood. Swami Vivekananda said in 1893 at the World's Parliament of Religions in Chicago: "I'm proud to belong to a religion that has taught the world both tolerance and universal acceptance." A Hindu's religion is of universal nature, *Vasudhaiva Kutumbakam*, encompassing the whole earth. The Aryans who migrated to India and settled beyond Sindhu became Hindu. And Hinduism implies the totality of religious forms which originated and developed on Indian soil. It is *Sanatana Dharma*—Eternal Law or Essence. It has always been there. Nobody can say when it was born or who was its founder.[41] There are founders for all other religions. Hinduism believes in the oneness and essential godliness of all beings. It is tolerant, without the kind of conversions resorted to by Christianity and Islam through enticement or coercion. In *Following the Equator*, Mark Twain objects to what he calls the "missionary trade" since its theological efforts are devoted to making people, especially children, traitors to the religion of their parents. He finds that some natives pretend to be Christian converts in order to gain material benefits from the White man. These "rice-Christians," as he calls them, are lazy and incompetent, no credit to the missionary effort. "Traitors to religion are of the same stuff as other traitors," Twain says, "the poorest material in camp."[42] As Swami Vivekananda said in an interview in 1899, "'When the Mohammedans first came, we are said to have been six hundred millions of Hindus. Now we are about two hundred millions...the vast majority of Hindu perverts to Islam and Christianity are perverts by the sword, or the descendants of these...."[43]

Referring to the secret of the great success of Hinduism, Mahatma Gandhi said in his speech on "The Spirit of Hinduism" on October 20, 1927 at Trivandrum:

> The Hindu civilization has survived the Egyptian, the Assyrian and the Babylonian. The Christian is but two thousand years old. The Islamic is but of yesterday. Great as both these are they are still, in my humble opinion, in the making.[44]

In the process of "making," Islam and Christianity resorted to dubious methods of conversions to increase their numbers, taking advantage of the Hindu tolerance. According to Brian Brown,

> In fact, between the years 1500 and 500 B.C., the people of India were so far advanced in religion, metaphysics, philosophy, science, art, music, and medicine, that no other nation could stand as their rival, or compete with them in any of these branches of knowledge.[45]

Indians in general, and a majority of them, Hindus in particular, deriving strength from the rich cultural heritage, have been excelling today in all these branches of knowledge, more specifically Information Technology, providing mature leadership to the rest of the world. A.L. Basham in *The Wonder That Was India* (1954) makes an extensive survey of the ancient Indian civilization before the coming of the Muslims.[46] This richness of the ancient Indian culture, which Naipaul has been at pains to make the world realize, constitutes the backdrop of his scrutiny of the Indian subcontinent ever since he wrote *An Area of Darkness.* The preeminence of the Indian civilization has not been adequately comprehended even by many Indians.

Naipaul expresses deep sympathy for the majority Hindus for being exploited not only by the foreign invaders like Muslims and Christians but also by the "secularist" opportunists of post-Independence India. This expression of sympathy on his part is in the same degree as his contempt for lethargy, insanitary conditions, and official apathy.

India with its Hindu majority has been pluralistic like America with its Christian majority. America tolerates the multiple religions of the ethnic groups and India too has been cosmopolitan without resorting to proselytizing. In a recent article titled "Two Concepts of Secularism" in *Wilson Quarterly,* Wilfred M. McClay says that while Secularism in America is anti-religious world-view imposed by the state, in India it is anti-theocratic understanding of a secular state with religious liberty.[47] Hinduism is, by its ideal of tolerance, has been secular, whatever the government in power. Naipaul has obviously noticed during his recent visits to India the outbursts of the pseudo-secularists against what is called "Hindu fundamentalism." However, fundamentalism of the kind present in the proselytizing religions results from obscurantism. As S. Radhakrishnan says in an article "An Indian Approach to Religion," "By the use of reason, Indian religious thought strives to rid religion of obscurantism."[48] That is the true secular base of Hinduism. Naipaul has noticed the spontaneous reaction of the majority Hindus, their decades of tolerance having been stretched to a breaking point. There seems to be a widespread overt and covert support of the silent majority to the "Hindutva" resurgence of the present times. Hinduism, with its secular base, does not undermine the Indian pluralism or multiculturalism. Hindutva is a way of life of the Indian people at large.[49] Like the Westerners generally, Naipaul had been earlier confused by the Indian attitude of resignation. But subsequently he has been convinced that the real strength of the Hindu mind lies in its rootedness, its tolerance and stoicism in the face of upheavals. Hindus believe that the actions of the previous birth affect one's life of the present, destined by Fate. Even the Westerners cannot escape the past despite all their materialism. In the Christian concept of Fall, the sin of the first man eating the Forbidden Fruit would visit upon all humans for ever. While the Christian idea of Original Sin is tragic in implication, the Hindu concept of Karma is stoic. The Lord's exhortation in *Bhagavad Gita, "karmanyevaadhikaraste, maa phaleshu kada chana"* (you have a right only for action, not its result) signifies that the Karma doctrine is action-oriented, giving stability to the mind. Naipaul has acknowledged the importance of this even for himself.

It will be interesting to know what Pravrajika Vrajapana of the Vedanta Society's Sarada Convent in Santa Barbara, California says:

> Post-September 11, everything has been different.... Our largest attendance for a lecture ever occurred the Sunday after 11.... The vast majority of the people were westerners. The biggest change that we can see here is the centrality that both the family and religion in general has taken. Both had been given short shrift in American society and it took a tragedy of this magnitude for people to realize that they had wilfully starved themselves of what gives life deeper meaning.[50]

It is this shock-absorbing nature of Hinduism with its Karma doctrine and the familial bonds which Naipaul recognizes as central to the culture of his ancestors. He continues to be deeply attached to his family in Port of Spain, looking back to the distant ancestry. In *An Area of Darkness* as well as some of his subsequent publications and statements in India, Naipaul acknowledges the basic strength of the Indian mind which is also his own. And this indeed has been his cultural rediscovery in the course of his Indian odyssey.

NOTES

1. *India Today* (October 22, 2001) 52.
2. *The New Indian Express,* December 9, 2001.
3. Leon Gottfield, "A Skeptical Pilgrimage," *Modern Fiction Studies,* 30, iii (Autumn 1984) 57l.
4. V.S. Naipaul, *India: A Wounded Civilization* (London: Andre Deutech, 1977) 9.
5. John Thieme, "A Hindu Castaway: Ralph Singh's Journey in The Mimic Men," *Modern Fiction Studies,* 30, iii (Autumn 1984) 508.
6. Rahul Singh, "Nobel Finally Comes Naipaul's Way," *Sovereign* (November 200l) 22.
7. Nissim Ezekiel, "Naipaul's India and Mine," *Indian English Prose: An Anthology,* ed. D. Ramakrishna (New Delhi: Arnold-Heinemann, 1980) 126-43.
8. Leon Gottfield 571.
9. Gita Hariharan, "The Ignoble Politics of Naipaul's Nobel," *Frontline,* 18, 23 (November 10-23, 2001) 70.
10. *Ibid.*
11. V.S. Naipaul, *An Area of Darkness* (1964; rpt. Harmondsworth: Penguin Books Ltd., 1968) 187-88.
12. John Thieme 508.
13. Philip Gourevitch, "Naipaul's World," *Commentary,* 98, 2 (August 1994) 29.
14. John Thieme 518.
15. V.S. Naipaul, *The Mimic Men* (London: Andre Deutsch, 1967) 300.
16. *The Sunday Express,* March 3, 2002.
17. Bruce Bawer, "Civilization and V.S. Naipaul," *The Hudson Review,* LV, 3 (Autumn 2002) 382.
18. *The Sunday Express,* March 3, 2002.

19. V.S. Naipaul, *In a Free State* (London: Andre Deutsche, 1971) 255.
20. Malcolm Jones, "A Voice for Dire Times," *Newsweek* (October 2001) 50.
21. Stephen Schiff, "The Ultimate Exile," *The New Yorker* (May 23, 1994) 61.
22. V.S. Naipaul, *A Way in the World* (London: Heinemann, 1994) 9.
23. "Bleeding Ink," *Outlook* (March 2, 2002) 56.
24. Stephen Schiff 61.
25. V.S. Naipaul, "Prologue," *Beyond Belief: Islamic Excursions Among the Converted People* (New Delhi: Penguin Books, 1998) 2.
26. V.S. Naipaul, *Beyond Belief* 2.
27. Stephen Schiff 70.
28. Stephen Schiff 62.
29. Khushwant Singh, "Nobelity at Last," *Outlook,* XLI, 39 (October 22, 2001) 18.
30. Gita Hariharan 70.
31. Gita Hariharan 72.
32. S. Prasannarajan, "A Prize for Sir Vidia," *India Today* (October 22, 2001) 52.
33. V.S. Naipaul, *Beyond Belief* 72.
34. Khushwant Singh 18.
35. Malcolm Jones 50.
36. *Ibid.*
37. Khushwant Singh 18.
38. V.S. Naipaul, *India: A Wounded Civilization* 48.
39. V.S. Naipaul, *India: A Million Mutinies Now* (1990; rpt. London: Vintage, 1998) 4. Further references to this text are given in parentheses.
40. Samuel P. Huntington, *The Clash of Civilizations and the Remaking of World Order* (New York: Simon & Schuster, 1996).
41. Maintaining that Hinduism dates back to the period between the sixth and fourth centuries B.C., Louis Renou says:
    Hinduism is indeed a complex and rich religion. No founder's initiative, no dogma, no reform have imposed restrictions on its domain; on the contrary, the contributions of the centuries have been superimposed without ever wearing out the previous layers of development.
    Louis Renou, ed., *Hinduism* (London: Prentice-Hall International, 1961) 17.
42. Mark Twain, *Following the Equator: A Journey Around the World* (1897; rpt. New York: Harper & Brothers Publishers, 1925).

43. *The Complete Works of Swami Vivekananda* (Calcutta: Advaita Asrama, 1989) v, 233.
44. M.K. Gandhi, *Young India* 419.
45. Brian Brown, *The Wisdom of the Hindus* (Delhi: Heritage Publishers, 1973) xxv.
    To the Western world, India has been a land of mystery, a land full of unintelligible systems of beliefs and puzzling philosophies. As Brown says, "Centuries before Plato wrote, or Pericles ruled, they ['the Hindus'] had a practical system of government; while in the sphere of philosophy they rose to a height of speculation attained by few of the later Europeans. They were, for example, among the first of the races to proclaim the brotherhood of man" (xxi).
46. A.L. Basham, *The Wonder That Was India* (1954; New Delhi: Rupa & Co., 1967).
47. Wilfred M. McClay, "Two Concepts of Secularism," (2000; rpt. SPAN, xlii, i (Jan-Feb 2001) 10.
48. S. Radhakrishnan, *The Present Crisis of Faith* (Delhi: Hind Pocket Books (P.) Ltd., I960) 40.
49. In view of the recent hullabaloo "regarding Hindutva or Hinduism, it will be interesting to see what the Supreme Court has said: "...the words 'Hinduism' or 'Hindutva' are not necessarily to be understood and construed narrowly confined only to the strict Hindu religious practices unrelated to the culture and ethos of the people of India, depicting the way of life of the Indian people."

    See M. Rama Jois, *Supreme Court Judgment on "Hindutva": An Important Land Mark* (New Delhi: Suruchi Prakashan, 1996) 59.
50. "In Search of Spirituality," *The Week* (June 30, 2002) 82.